ALL NEW SQUARE FOOT GARDENING

WITH KIDS

Learn Together:

- Gardening basics
- Science and math
- Water conservation
- Self-sufficiency
- Healthy eating

MEL BARTHOLOMEW

First published in 2014 by Cool Springs Press, an imprint of the Quarto Publishing Group USA Inc.,400 First Avenue North, Suite 400, Minneapolis, MN 55401

Cool Springs Press titles are also available at discounts in bulk quantity for industrial or sales-promotional use. For details write to Special Sales Manager at Quarto Publishing Group USA Inc.,400 First Avenue North, Suite 400, Minneapolis, MN 55401 USA. To find out more about our books, visit us online at www.coolspringspress.com.

Library of Congress Cataloging-in-Publication Data

Bartholomew, Mel.

 Square foot gardening with kids : learn together : gardening basics : science and math, water conservation, self-sufficiency, healthy eating / Mel Bartholomew.

    p. cm.

 Includes index.

 ISBN 978-1-59186-594-0 (sc)

 1. Vegetable gardening. 2. Square foot gardening. 3. Gardening for children. I. Title.

SB321.B284 2014

635--dc23

OCLC   12/2014

                    2013039020

Acquisitions Editor: Mark Johanson

Design Manager: Brad Springer

Layout: Ryan Scheife, Mayfly Design

Special thanks to our Junior Square Foot Gardeners who helped out with this book:

Ava Dilley, Eli Dilley, Aspen Danielle Foy, Autumn Glory Foy, Nate Gilg, Chloe Laun, Luke Laun, Anna Lukens, Graham Markert, Leo Pernu, Cole Schiele, David Sutch

Printed in China

10 9 8 7 6 5 4 3 2

Table of Contents

Introduction to Square Foot Gardening with Kids

Hi, I'm Mel Bartholomew, the founder of Square Foot Gardening, and I'm happy to have written this new book. I've been meaning to write a book on gardening with kids ever since I started teaching Square Foot Gardening almost forty years ago. The reason is simple: kids love to play in the dirt and watch their plants grow into food. In fact, kids have always been my best and most enthusiastic students.

Square Foot Gardening is more than just another activity to entertain children. It is also an ideal way for parents, grandparents, teachers, and leaders to teach a million useful lessons on practically every imaginable subject. If you are looking for a way to learn, have fun, and bond with the youngsters in your life, you won't find a better, healthier, more positive (and fun!) vehicle than building, planting, and harvesting an SFG together.

Square Foot Gardening with Kids is all about kids and gardening, but it is written mostly for adults because you are the ones who will be doing most of the teaching. In the pages that follow, you're going to find lots and lots of ideas for how to get kids involved with a Square Foot Garden, and how to teach them lessons from math, to reading and writing, to art. Just keep in mind that you know your child—and yourself—best. If math in the garden isn't going to fly and might turn your kids off, well then move on to another subject. Sometimes, you don't need anything more than to be teaching children the value of growing their own food and the simple pleasure of getting out in the garden and being a part of nature. But however you choose to engage your kids, you're going to find plenty of examples of how to approach different learning and life subjects through the teaching lens of Square Foot Gardening.

Building, planting, tending, and harvesting your own kid-sized Square Foot Gardening box is a fun and rewarding project for kids as well as adults.

What Is Square Foot Gardening?

I developed the idea of Square Foot Gardening 40 years ago and I have spent most of my time since then talking about it and teaching it to new Square Foot Gardeners. I have a lot to say about it—not just about how it is done, but also about how much good it can do in the world. You'll figure this out pretty quickly as you read through my book. But having said that, *Square Foot Gardening with Kids* is specifically about kids and teaching and learning and having fun. I'll give you enough information about the method as we go along that you can teach the material. But if you're new to the method and are serious about learning all the intricacies and benefits, you'll need to look somewhere else. May I suggest the second edition of All *New Square Foot Gardening* that we published in 2013?

Following is a concise introduction to the nuts and bolts (and some of the whys) that anyone starting a Square Foot Garden needs to know.

My book, *All New Square Foot Gardening*, will answer practically any question you might have about the SFG method. It is a good background source, but you and your kids can easily make your own kid-size box and garden using just the information you find in *Square Foot Gardening with Kids*.

A kid-size Square Foot Garden is a simple planting box that's 3-ft. square and is divided into 1-ft. planting grids (the full-sized version is a 4 x 4-ft. box with 16 squares).

The Simplest—and Best—Gardening Method

Before you start teaching or learning anything with SFG, you need to know the basics of the method. Thank goodness the method was very simple to start with, and I refined it recently to make even simpler. I like to say that Square Foot Gardening is as much about what you don't need, as what you do need. With SFG, you don't need a lot of room in your backyard, you don't need good soil, you don't need backbreaking work constantly digging and weeding, you don't need tools, and you don't need fertilizer, pesticides, or insecticides. SFG is an all-natural, organic way to garden. You won't need a lot of time, and you won't need aspirin—because you're not going to be doing the type of digging and weeding or other traditional gardening work that makes you exhausted and sore. That simplicity is what makes SFG the perfect activity to do with kids. Even young ones will understand the basics right away, and because they won't be digging and weeding half the day under the hot sun, they'll enjoy it and stick with it.

In an SFG, a raised planting box is filled with a special soil blend and divided into 1-ft. squares. Each square in (nine in a children's box and 16 in a full-size box) is planted with a different vegetable, herb, or flower. Depending on how much space the mature plant needs, you may grow anywhere from 1 to 16 plants in any given square. Because the soil is all new, almost no weeding is needed. It's mostly just water and wait.

A Square Foot Garden takes all the work out of gardening—no digging, no weeding, no kidding! A simple, easy way to grow fresh, tasty food.

SFG and Schools

I wrote this book with the idea that it would be read by parents, teachers, and older kids so you can share the ideas with younger children. I know this works as a way of teaching because I have seen it work well so many times. One of the best examples I've run across is the story of a public school teacher who taught every school class subject by using her SFG, including history, science, and art. Do you know how she started and got the kids interested in learning every subject from their garden? She began by gathering all her students, sitting them down on the floor around her, and reading to them from my first SFG book. Now, these were six- and seven-year-olds. Then, they built their own school SFG, and each student took possession of their very own SFG square and away they went on an adventure of learning. You could do the same with this book. It will give you some valuable insights and expand on the basics, and will help you and your children get the most out of SFG.

I've watched as school districts across the country have adopted Square Foot Gardening into the schoolyard as a way to teach children many different lessons on every subject they study in school. I can tell you, I've had some pretty wonderful moments touring schoolyards where kids proudly displayed their Square Foot Gardens. You can't get a word in edgewise when those youngsters start talking about all the produce they've grown and all the new things they've learned—they talk a mile a minute because they're so excited about it. And I don't even think they realize everything they're learning, because SFG makes learning just plain fun.

Building, planting, and harvesting SFG boxes is a fun activity for schools and kids programs, too. You can use an SFG to teach just about any subject you can think of—math is an obvious one, but history, biology, and certainly resource management can be taught inside the box.

SFG, The Condensed Version

Growing an SFG with children involves a slightly smaller box than an adult would use, but everything else is the same. That means you can use all the information that follows for your own and your kids' Square Foot Gardens. Here's a quick crash course on the method.

The Box

Square Foot Gardening starts with a special square box that sits on top of your existing soil, or pretty much anywhere else you want to put it. The box allows for easy access, and will contain everything you need for growing your Square Foot Garden, including the soil. You can even put a plywood bottom on the box and make it portable. For adults, the standard SFG box is 4 feet by 4 feet and 6 inches deep. It's divided into 16 equal squares (the "Square Feet" in the title) with a grid laid on top of the soil. I selected this box size based on how far people can comfortably reach in to tend their gardens without falling into it or stepping on the soil. Children are smaller and can't reach quite as far, which is why we build children's SFG boxes 3 feet by 3 feet (but still 6 inches deep). At the Square Foot Gardening Foundation, we call this the "Square Yard" box, and we developed it for our "Square Yard in the School Yard" program.

SFG boxes can be made of any material that doesn't contain contaminants like preservatives or paint. You name it, I've seen boxes built of it. But I prefer to use wood, and especially wood I get for free, left over from construction projects. You can also take a shortcut and buy premade, ready-to-assemble boxes right from the Square Foot Gardening Foundation's website at www.squarefootgardening.org. That's how we raise money for our educational and humanitarian projects.

Now you might say, "Wait a minute Mel. How is that small box going to produce enough vegetables to be worth the effort?" Well, that's the beauty of an SFG. It takes less water, less soil, fewer seeds, no fertilizer, and no work to produce a much greater yield than the same amount of space in a traditional row garden. Actually five times the harvest of a row garden in the same space.

The kid-size SFG box is smaller than the full-size version so children can reach all the way into the middle of it.

Super Soil

We don't use the soil in your yard for a Square Foot Garden, because the fact is, most people's soil is pretty poor. That's why row gardeners are stuck with having to test their soil, dig it up every spring, and add the fertilizers, bags of compost, and all kinds of other stuff. Yikes, that's a lot of hard work and they do it every spring! So instead, your child's SFG box will be filled with a very special soil we call Mel's Mix, and it's equal parts by volume of compost blend (ideally, five or more different types of compost), peat moss or coir, and coarse vermiculite. I created it especially to provide the perfect loose, workable, and nutritious soil, and one that has holds just enough water to keep your plants healthy. Plants don't dry out in Mel's Mix and every drop of water is put to good use.

I formulated Mel's Mix to have a more-or-less neutral pH. This is a measure of the balance of acid to alkaline in the soil, and neutral pH is just about perfect for most garden plants. Best of all, it means you don't need to add anything to Mel's Mix to get your plants growing like crazy.

You can make your own batch of Mel's Mix and it's the last time you'll need to fuss with the soil. It will last for about 10 years with just a handful of compost added to each square each time you harvest and replant that square.

Mel's Mix not only gives your plants the best possible start, it also saves you work because you never need to dig it up, amend it, or fertilize. SFG is all natural and organic. The soil has no weed seeds, so your children will never have to weed their SFG. Ask them how they'll feel about that!

The super soil used in an SFG is a blend of equal volumes of peat moss, compost, and vermiculite called "Mel's Mix." You dump all the ingredients into a wheelbarrow or onto a tarp and mix them up. Pretty simple.

Planning & Planting

Deciding on what to plant in an SFG is just about the most fun your kids will ever have in the garden. There are so many possibilities! The best approach is to plant something different in every square of any given SFG box, but beyond that, the sky's the limit. Some plants like to be together, like several squares of corn together. Most plants can be all by themselves in their separate square of the grid.

Speaking of that grid, it's actually a grid. I tell people if you don't have a grid, you don't have a Square Foot Garden. The grid we put on top of the soil in the box—and attach to the box itself—outlines each square and keeps things neat and tidy.

The grid is necessary to help us organize the plants in the SFG box. We think of plants like shirt sizes; they come in:

Extra large = 1 per square
Large = 4 per square
Medium = 9 per square
Small = 16 per square

Depending on the plant in that square, you divide up the square in into that number of smaller squares. Can you just see all the possibilities for teaching fractions?

I have a special—and especially fun—way for children to mark the smaller squares in their SFG. I call it Zip, Zap, Bing, Bing, Bing, Bing. You'll find it described on page 82—it's a great trick to help even very young

"Zip, Zap, Bing, Bing, Bing, Bing" is a kid-friendly method for spacing seeds.

children plant in a uniform grid without fussing about too much, and there is no measuring to do. Kids just love it (and it works for adults too).

. . . .

Keep a full bucket of water near your SFG box, preferably in the sunshine. Dip into the bucket when your plants are thirsty and give them a drink.

. . . .

Growing Your Garden

Because the Mel's Mix in your SFG is brand-new soil, there is practically zero weeding required. As the plants grow, they are going to need water of course, and we make watering simple. Fill a 5-gallon bucket with water and place it next to each box. Drop a small plastic cup in the bucket and bingo, you've got your watering system.

The idea is that kids can water their plants whenever the soil dries out, and they should check the soil every day. Teach your kids to treat plants like children. If it's hot outside and a child would need a drink, their plants probably do too! How much? Depends on the size of the child or plant. Big kids get a big drink, etc. See the logic of SFG?

Keeping the water bucket right by the SFG box makes watering easy, but it also ensures that plants get wonderful, sun-warmed water.

Whether it's a cantaloupe, a tomato, or a carrot... picking a ripe veggie you grew yourself feels like opening a gift on a holiday morning... only better, because you've accomplished something magical.

Harvesting

There is nothing quite like the look on a child's face when she picks the very first tomato she's ever grown. It's plump and red, and sure to be juicy, and it's all hers. That pure joy is what makes harvesting the Square Foot Garden a favorite time for me, and for all the children who have put in the effort and grown their very own SFGs. All their work is paying off (even if it was more like play than work)!

As the garden matures, there are many chances to teach children how to get the most out of their plants. They'll also need to learn when a fruit or vegetable is ripe, and how best to harvest crops without damaging the plants. Of course, older kids can learn ways to get even more out of their Square Foot Gardens, with crop rotation and vertical gardening. So let's learn how to make the most of those gardens!

Getting the Most Out of This Book

Square Foot Gardening is a wonderful way to bring the whole family together in a positive, healthy, productive activity. And you should see the chests puff out as kids pull up their very first carrot or pick the first tomato that they grew themselves. It gives them so much confidence and self-esteem. They will, of course, want to eat everything they grow, so they'll be eating healthier as well. And as you'll see as you read on, making and planting an SFG is just about a perfect way to teach kids of all ages about science, ecology, math, design, and even art, language, and logic—not to mention gardening and self-sufficiency.

Keeping kids interested is not a problem with a Square Foot Garden. Because they'll be growing so much in such a small space, there's always something new and interesting popping up. Kids come to understand that SFG is more like play than work. It's an enjoyable way for them to get outside and move around, and it's an ideal way for you to spend time with your kids—especially if you have a full-size box of your own. In fact, it's a super idea for you to have your own box. There's no better way to get children involved than by setting a good example. And how often do you get to be that close with your kids in an enjoyable setting?

But basically, that's the whole SFG process in a nutshell. Build a box, fill it with Mel's Mix, put a grid on top, decide on the plants, plant them, grow them, and harvest them. Didn't I tell you it was easy? Along the way, nobody will need to weed, dig, amend, or do any hard work—that would just get in the way of learning and having fun. The kids just check their plants regularly, make sure the plants aren't being bothered by insects, and pick the harvest when it's ready.

Your kids' SFG box can be plain and functional, bright and colorful, or customized with all the SFG accessories. Deciding how to approach it together is a big part of the fun.

Tips for Gardening with Kids

I've introduced quite a few children to the SFG method over the years, so here are a few tips and suggestions for success that I have picked up along the way.

- **Start modestly.** There's no need to fill your whole yard with SFG boxes and that wouldn't be a good thing even if you could. Kids should grow only what you're sure they can and will eat, or can easily give away. Remember, SFG isn't work, and you don't want to make it seem like that. Best to start with just one 3 x 3 box per child for the first season. Schools allot just one square per student. Next season, you can add a box if the kids want it and ask for it.

- **Involve the child.** Every step along the way, from reading the book, to building the SFG box, planting, growing, nurturing, to the final harvest, represents a chance for kids to be involved, have fun and learn. If you're patient, kids of any age can help build boxes, mix Mel's Mix, and participate in every aspect of Square Foot Gardening. Even if they can't do everything themselves, don't do it for them. Give them whatever help they need to create a Square Foot Garden they can rightfully call their own.

- **Reinforce the benefits.** When your child comes running into the house with a squash she grew in her Square Foot Garden, don't just pat her on the head and say, "That's nice dear." Get excited too. Find a good recipe for squash soup or squash au gratin and cook it that very night so that your little Square Foot Gardener understands how valuable her harvest is.

- **Look for lessons.** A Square Foot Garden is a wonderful teacher. Use it as a tool, but pick the lessons that won't dampen children's enthusiasm. Build on teachable moments as they come along and SFG will always be fun and rewarding for you *and* your children.

- **Share.** Kids love to share their successes, and you can help them do that with their SFG. Get grandma and grandpa on the phone (or, better yet, on a video chat!) to let them know what's growing. It's a great way for grandparents and grandkids to connect. Invite your child's friends over for a garden party and help your child decorate her SFG. Sharing is part of the great fun and adventure of Square Foot Gardening—even for adults!

- **Fun.** Most of all, have fun. Square Foot Gardening has changed millions of lives, and if the letters I get are any indication, the thing that most impresses people when they start Square Foot Gardening is how much they just plain enjoy it. Dive into the chapters that follow, and I think you're going to find out just how enjoyable Square Foot Gardening with Kids can be!

Of all the reasons to enjoy gardening with your kids, perhaps none is more important than simply spending time together.

Kids and SFG Go Together Like Carrots & Tomatoes

You'd be amazed at how children—even toddlers two and three years old—take to gardening. But if you want to get them really involved and engaged, the type of garden to start with is a Square Foot Garden, and the time to start is right at the beginning. Include your kids in the planning of their SFG. This chapter explains how to use this book to work with kids of all ages to plan out a Square Foot Garden that will make the most of your family time in your yard and yield harvests that make everyone excited. Like most everything else about Square Foot Gardening, the planning phase is a lot of fun and no work at all.

A box full of soil and the open road ahead? What could be more fun than that for kids of any age. And just wait until beautiful and delicious plants start to pop and grow. Your child will be amazed, and so will you.

Toddlers in the Square Foot Garden

Nothing makes me happier than seeing toddlers in the garden. Where parents see diapers to be changed, I see future Square Foot Gardeners! That's why I always tell parents that it's never too early to start children gardening. Sure, they may not garden quite like you do, but that doesn't mean they can't get out there and benefit from some quality time spent with an SFG.

It's all a matter of adapting a little bit and having some patience. You can start by making your SFG boxes attractive to the toddler. Some brightly colored paint on the outside of the box (let's just be sure to keep the paint on the outside, so the good stuff growing inside doesn't get contaminated) goes a long way to delighting little tykes. Look at seed catalogs and take the toddlers along on trips to the nursery. These little ones just love to see and touch pretty plants. You're also going to find out that toddlers just love—and I mean love—dirt. They like to play, dig, and stomp the dirt. That's not SFG; we treat our garden and all the plants like members of the family. Be kind and help them grow. That's why you'll want to keep toddlers out of the box once it's planted— it's not a sand box! It's best to give them something that will preoccupy them. A little plastic bucket full of Mel's Mix and a tiny plastic shovel can make a toddler feel like she's part of the whole gardening process. Or how about this 1 x 1 idea? Build a miniature 1-foot x 1-foot box with a bottom, fill it with Mel's Mix soil, and your toddler will have a manageable, carry-along garden.

Gardening can be even more fun with a crowd. Don't be afraid to get your child's friends, siblings, or even whole school class involved. Kids love to do things in packs, and there's nothing better for a pack of kids than a Square Foot Garden. You can even throw a birthday party around a 1 x 1 SFG box—have the kids plant it as part of the festivities!

In this chapter we're going to learn all about the SFG box. Why a box? It provides protection for your plants, and a border not to be crossed for one thing. Of course, it works both ways too: You can talk to your plants, "Now you guys stay in the box!" Along the way, we're going to see how much fun learning with an SFG can be. So let's get started!

Kids Are Not One Size

Wherever possible, we've tried to make all the information in this book work for kids of any age. One of the ways we do that is by making suggestions for interacting with kids who are in different age groups. The general age breakdowns for each group are listed to the right. Throughout this book, you'll come across many exercises and activities where we suggest age-sensitive variations of a core activity so you can customize the learning to your own kids' needs and interests. Just keep in mind that some kids may be more comfortable in a different group than their age would indicate. You know your child (or students) best, so use the information you think is most applicable for your Junior Square Foot Gardener.

 Preschool Growers = Ages 2 to 5

 Early Learners = Ages 6 to 9

 Terrific Tweens = Ages 10 to 13

 Cultivating Teens = Ages 14 and up

Using this book

Square Foot Gardening with Kids has enough information about gardening that you could use it as a basis for building and planting your own SFG. But as you read through the following chapters you will find a lot more than that. Around the basic SFG method I have wrapped dozens and dozens of lessons and activities for you to consider and share. Some "lessons" are just a quick question you can ask. Others are more like stories. And some are even like pop quizzes (no final exams though!). They are meant to help your kids think about new ideas and learn new things. And they are meant to help you and the child have fun together.

While some of the lessons in this book are simply mentioned as I write along, others have been categorized and pulled out in easy-to-find boxes. These boxes have been grouped into five categories for your convenience. They are:

Build Your Own   **Science Discovery**   **Fun with Art**
SFG Activity   **Math Blaster**

There is plenty of information in this book that doesn't fit into any of these categories. But that's Square Foot Gardening for you. The box might be a perfect square that's divided into uniform grids, but you never know what you'll find in each grid. An eggplant might show up next to some cilantro. A bunch of beets can be neighbors to a bed of marigolds. SFG isn't about putting everything into neat rows. So follow along with me and be prepared for some surprises.

FUN WITH ART:
A Sunny Exercise

Planning a garden starts with drawings. So it's time to find some big pieces of paper, and crayons or markers (rulers, compasses, and pencils for the Plants), and explore the sunlight out back (or wherever you think the garden will go). Kids like to see things in picture form because that's how they first understand concepts. It works even better when they make the picture themselves. So we're going to start the children off by having them draw pictures of possibilities to find the best place for the SFG box they will build.

◐ **Preschool Growers (2-5).** If you are working with very young Square Foot Gardeners, you simply want to reinforce the notion that sun is good for the plants. Have them draw a picture of where their SFG box might go and what it might look like when the plants are all grown up. Make sure they include a big, bright sun in the sky! Then, for a temporary marker, make a big X, and tell the child that X marks the spot like in a treasure map. Have the little one place the X where they think the garden would be best placed, and have them watch that point over the next three days to see what type of sun it gets (this will be a good lesson in patience and planning).

☀ **Early Learners (6-9).** Early Learners may be able to do a little bit more with their pictures. Ask them to draw the outline of their yard and color where the sunlight falls. Remember that you're just trying to get them to think about the best place to put their SFG box and what role weather and sun will play.

Challenge your young learners to find a way to draw how the sun moves across the sky in your yard. What does this tell us about placing our SFG box?

◑ **Terrific Tweens (10-13)** will be able to measure the yard and actually make a sketch to scale (just like an engineer!) with basic, proper dimensions. It doesn't have to be highly detailed, but ask them to put in all the features of the yard—trees, decks, a pool. Now where should the SFG box go? Where is the strongest and longest sunlight exposure? Is there somewhere to put it that you could see it from your bedroom window?

✿ **Cultivating Teens (14+).** If you're dealing with older kids, the sky's the limit. They can do a really detailed sketch by hand, or on the computer. How would you represent a tree? A circle. Good. How about a fence? How about a patio? Did you double-check your measurements? Where does the box go? Can we include more than one box if we want to (teaching thinking ahead to plan for future growth)? This is also the chance to talk about sun exposure over time. Have your teen check the yard at different times of the day and mark how the sunlight changes on their sketch. How can they show the sunlight on the ground for different times, say 9 a.m., noon, 4 p.m., and 7 p.m.? They can use one of two ways, with different lines slanted in different directions, or with different colors.

Teaching Moment: Sunlight, Explained

Plants are like us: they can't do without food. But plants need sunlight even more, because it helps them make their own food. Now that's amazing. I like to make that explanation as simple as possible for preschoolers: plants love sunlight, so let's put them in the sunlight whenever we can. Of course, they get thirsty too, so let's always be sure to give them water when it's hot or they will look a little wilted.

If you're a teacher or a parent with a grade school-age child, you can talk a little more about sunlight and plants. How do we get sunlight? Well, the earth is a great big ball and it spins around so that the sunlight hits any part of the Earth half the day. I used a flashlight and a softball to teach my granddaughter about how sunlight strikes the Earth.

Seed Catalogs

I like to get kids involved right from the start. The best way is to give them seed catalogs and let them discover all the things they could plant. Just about any seed company's website will allow you sign up for a seed catalog by mail. Here's an idea: If you have classroom full of kids or are gathering a group of neighborhood children, call the seed company directly and ask for several copies of their previous year's seed catalog. They're sure to have extra copies lying around, and it would be good promotion on their part!

The process of picking plants for the SFG gives you the chance to discuss species and varieties, growing times, seasons, pests, and more). Most important is to grow what you like to eat or what would be fun, while also learning which are the easiest plants to grow. You can talk to your kids about why we don't grow certain plants in an SFG (no trees or bushes please!), and what plants they would like to grow and why (radishes are always a favorite). The most crucial thing to discuss is why there is a grid in SFG and how many plants of a certain type can fit into one square foot. We give plants the room they need, but no more—there's no waste in an SFG, not even space!

. . . .

Supply the kids with a bunch of old seed catalogs. They have good information, they're fun to look at, and they're free.

. . . .

FUN WITH ART:
Making a Map

Pictures always work best for very young learners, so one of the most powerful ways to get 4 to 6-year-olds involved in planning an SFG is to draw a big Square Foot Garden box (9 squares in a grid) on a large sheet of sketch paper or a piece of poster board. Then have the children cut pictures of the plants they want to include out of seed catalogs. The kids will have a great time placing the pictures in the individual squares, and before they actually plant, they may find they want to rearrange some

Whether your child uses crayons, paint, markers, pencil, pens or even a computer, making a few drawings of the yard and some possible SFG locations is a good way to get the project started.

plants to a different square. Now you'll have a handy visual plan of what the children's SFG will look like. You can use this diagram to discuss how many plants go in each square, how long till they're ready, and much, much more! You might even be thinking of what will grow next in each square after it is harvested.

Reading Readiness

An index is a handy thing to know how to use. Why not take advantage of the seed or nursery catalog to explain to children of any age what an index is, how it works, and how it can help you find just about anything in a book or catalog (and you can start by explaining what alphabetizing means for very young children)? Have your kids look up in the index plants they want to investigate. Afterwards, have them spell the plants' names—you'll find they can even learn to spell when they use the index! Give them some names to practice with words like "radishes," "beans," "peas," and "zucchini."

Sun and Seasons

Why can't we grow our Square Foot Gardens in winter? That's always a good question to ask children when they are planning their gardens. You'd be surprised at the answers you're going to get, but most children, even very young children, know that it's just too darned dark and cold for most plants to grow. You might have a little bit different discussion if you live in Florida.

For younger kids, it's enough to know that our part of the Earth is farther from the sun in winter, so we receive less sunshine. Older children can think about why the days are shorter during winter, and you can ask teens to explore why the sun is lower in the sky in the winter and higher in summer. No need to go too far with this idea in the planning stage. It's just important to have kids understand that the growing season is limited, and that we should keep that in mind when we decide on which plants we'll include in our SFG box.

Let's Choose Our Plants!

Notice that we don't say, "pick our plants," because you have to choose them and plant them *before* you pick them. Oh boy, do kids have fun with this! Choosing plants is when children can clearly see what they're going to harvest and eat. It's like peeking into the future.

Fun with Art

Children should make a list of the plants they want to include in their gardens, but lists are boring. Why not turn it into a chance to make art? Remember, 9 squares means 9 types of plants. Younger kids may not be able to write in the names of the plants, in which case they can cut out a picture or draw a picture in a square on the chart. Older kids can get a little funky and make stylized drawings or computer renditions of the plants, along with cool labels. When they're done, they'll not only have a plan for what and where they'll be growing in their SFG box, they'll have a wonderful artwork that might look absolutely stunning on the refrigerator or the door to a child's bedroom.

The Special Case of Flowers

If they've been paying attention, kids will notice that most of what we plant in an SFG is edible. It makes sense to get the most out of your garden, and planting vegetables, herbs, and edible plants is a good way to do just that. But when I work with kids, I like to have them plant a flowering annual (or perennial) in at least one square. Why? Well sometimes it's just nice to have something "perty" in the box. Say it just like that and your kids are sure to understand.

It's good to explain to older kids, or any child who doesn't see the value of including something they can't eat, that flowers attract insects that are necessary for the other plants to grow healthy and strong. But usually, kids love the idea of growing something "perty" and you don't need to ask them twice to select a flower for their SFG.

Kid-Favorites & Plant Spacing

I've helped more kids plant child-size Square Foot Gardens than I can count. In schools, community gardens and their own backyards, they all seem to be attracted to certain plants that just tickle the young imagination.

The number of seeds or plants you should plant in a square foot grid depends on the size of the plant when it is mature. Basically, they fall into the categories of small (16 per square), medium (9 per square), large (4 per square), and extra large (1 per square). Cut out pictures of these vegetables from a seed catalog or make photocopies of the ones on these pages.

This spacing relates to the "thin to" spacing requirements listed on the seed packets: 12-inch spacing equals 1 plant per square; 6-inch spacing equals 4 plants per square; 4-inch spacing equals 9 plants per square; and 3-inch spacing equals 16 plants per square. A head of cabbage is an example of an extra large plant that would take up a whole square. Leaf lettuces are planted 4 to a square, while beets are 9 to a square and radishes are 16 to a square.

Radish. 16 per square

Radishes. These are quick satisfaction for children because the seeds are large and easy to handle, they grow fast (harvest in 4 weeks) and there are lots of interesting varieties and colors that kids can choose from—even striped radishes or Easter egg colors! Plus, it's quite a treat for a kid to pull one up, wash it in the bucket of sun-warmed water and pop it in their mouth. It's a much better snack than potato chips.

Carrots. 16 per square

Carrots. Lots and lots to choose from, and kids just delight in the orange color. Grow ball carrots for a really fun treat that kids are sure to gobble up—there's no better way to get them to eat their vegetables! These first two vegetables have a hidden secret. The eating part is buried under ground, so it's a big surprise when you harvest them. Anticipation is the name of the game.

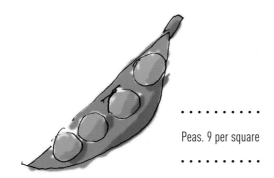

Peas. 9 per square

Bush beans. 9 per square

Snap peas. We grow these up on a support in an SFG and they produce crowds of pods to harvest. The little ones just love to eat them picked fresh. Who could blame them? So do the adults.

Bush Beans. Once they get gardening, kids want to reach in and work with their SFG. Bush beans tickle the hands when you water them and offer healthy harvests every kid can enjoy. Watching the blossoms turn into miniature beans is a wonder; they grow bigger and bigger every day.

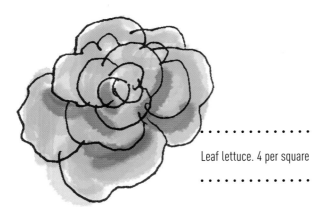

Leaf lettuce. 4 per square

Sunflowers. 1 per square

Leaf lettuces. Think kids don't like salad? Try planting a leaf lettuce and see what happens. Youngsters love that you continually harvest this vegetable all through the growing season, and they want to eat what they harvest.

Sunflowers. Maybe these aren't the most practical plants for a Square Foot Garden but kids just love to watch the pretty flowers turn to greet the sun. And what kid doesn't like cracking sunflower seeds between their teeth?

Cherry tomatoes. 1 per square

Cherry Tomatoes. I think the reason kids love this type of tomato so much is that it's bite sized and fits perfectly in a child's hand. Whatever the reason, children just seem to gravitate right to them in a Square Foot Garden.

Marigold. 4 per square

Marigolds. Simple as pie to grow, these brightly colored little flowers add a lot of beauty to a child's SFG box .

Broccoli: 1 per square

Broccoli. Not at the top of many kids' favorite veggies list, the broccoli is still a fun plant to grow—and maybe if your kid grew it herself she'll be more likely to eat and enjoy it.

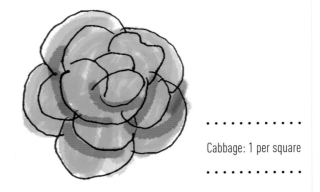

Cabbage: 1 per square

Cabbage. Another veggie most kids think is more fun to grow than to eat. But try reminding your child about cole slaw. Or sauerkraut (if you think that will help).

Peppers: 1 per square

Peppers. Red, green, and yellow bell peppers are very fun to watch grow and produce, and in most gardens they will make plenty of bright, colorful peppers that are a delight to pick and to eat.

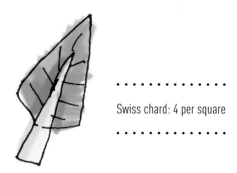

Swiss chard: 4 per square

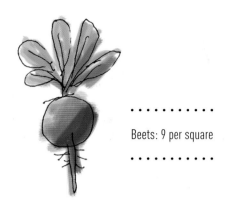

Beets: 9 per square

Swiss chard. These deep green (or rainbow) colored members of the cole family are beautiful and about as packed with vitamins as any vegetable you can think of.

Beets. Beets are a great plant for helping your kids understand the difference between roots and tubers. Beets are roots; potatoes are tubers. Beets are also yummy and earthy (but not everyone agrees).

Spinach: 9 per square

Onions: 16 per square

Spinach. A fine cool season grower, spinach comes in fast and early and can be replanted in late summer for a Fall harvest. Kids don't like spinach? One word: Popeye.

Onions. Red or yellow or white, onions are easy to grow and harvest. If you plan to store them, let them cure in the sun for a few days after you pick them, then move them to a cool, dry spot.

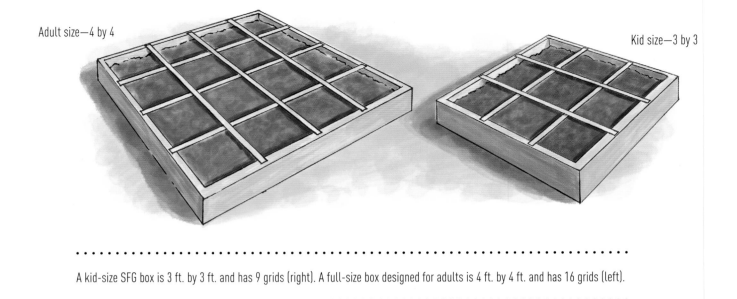

Adult size—4 by 4

Kid size—3 by 3

A kid-size SFG box is 3 ft. by 3 ft. and has 9 grids (right). A full-size box designed for adults is 4 ft. by 4 ft. and has 16 grids (left).

Start with the Box

Whether your children are 4 or 14, they'll start their SFG adventure by learning about the SFG box and the "squares." This is your chance to clearly explain the basic ideas behind planting a Square Foot Garden. A children's SFG box measures 3 feet by 3 feet, and always has nine squares: one type of plant per square, nine different kinds of plants per box.

Now kids are curious and they're sure to ask, "Why a square box, and why nine squares? Why not 10 or 15? Isn't more better?" It is because I tried out many different shapes in figuring out the Square Foot Gardening method, and a square is the best for spacing in the most plants in the smallest area without crowding. First, I measured how far children can reach into a box to tend plants,

and it turns out that 18 inches is about the farthest a youngster can reach in without falling into the box. You'll want to take care of the plants from all sides of the box by reaching in, so that means 9 individual 1-foot squares is just right. Any boy or girl can comfortably reach into the center of his or her box to take care of his or her plants. Every SFG box is also six inches deep, which leaves just enough room for the plants' roots without making the box unnecessarily deep and heavy. Did you notice how we use the initials "SFG" for the Square Foot Gardening method? That can be a good starting point to discuss abbreviations and how they work. Abbreviations can lead you all kinds of places with children—for instance, discussing the IRS, or ABC or PBS TV channels. Quiz them on what some common abbreviations stand for and ask them why we use abbreviations at all.

I tell children to think of the box as a house for their Square Foot Garden. Because, like any home, it's where the plants will be safe, and where kids will keep all the food and water their plants need to grow big and strong.

If your kids are like most, they will quickly figure out that an SFG box takes up very little space in a yard. Everyone gets excited when they started planning a garden, especially when that garden is a Square Foot Garden. And nobody gets more excited than children. So chances are that they may say, "If one box is good, how about two?" The fact is, the number of boxes you plant should be determined by the number of people in your house and size of the harvest you want. First, let's start with the idea that smaller is better for the environment, so we don't waste. I tell people to expect that a single SFG box will provide enough produce for one salad, for one person, every day during the growing season.

You may already have an adult-size 4-foot x 4-foot SFG box, or maybe you're planning your own so that you can have family boxes. Good for you, that's a great idea! But where children are concerned, their excitement can get the better of them. That's why I always start kids out with one box. It will be more than enough to tend and learn all about Square Foot Gardening (and lots of other lessons as well) and it will keep things fun and exciting for short attention spans. They can always add a second box the next growing season.

Mel's challenge: *Get your kids to think ahead a year or two, when they will be big enough to reach in 2 feet and can graduate to a 4 x 4 "adult" box. Then how many squares will there be? And what is so special about an adult-size box? Hint: How many square shapes are in a 4 x 4 box, and how does that relate to the square or square root sequence?*

Assembling the SFG Box is one of the most exciting moments when you're making your very own garden.

Making Your Own Box

For most kids, building their own SFG box brings gardening to life. They see up close where all their plants will live and grow. And by building their own box, they learn a little something about independence and achievement.

Building an SFG box of any size is actually pretty simple. It doesn't have any complicated corners or anything else to slip you up, it can be made from all kinds of materials (your child might even be able to find what he or she needs out back right now) and the construction is simple enough for even young children to handle. Kids just love to work with building supplies of any sort. In fact, it's good to let small children do as much of the work as possible and practical (making sure that they're safe, of course) and you'll be amazed at how proud they are of their very own SFG box. The more they help out in actually building the box, the more connected they become to the garden and all the good lessons it has to teach them. If you've got a teen or two on your hand, they can probably build a box all by themselves. Let them make any mistakes they might need to make, because there's no better way to build confidence and learn self-sufficiency than by fixing your own problems.

Math Blaster

Let's measure

Parents and teachers alike wind up amazed at how many practical skills Square Foot Gardening can teach children. It's not just how to grow food, although that's pretty darn important and it's the ultimate goal. Along the way, there is opportunity after opportunity for fun while teaching children basic life skills and knowledge that will serve them well throughout their lives. One of the most fundamental of these is measuring things.

Preschool Growers (2–5). Start out on the right foot by just getting them familiar with the basic concepts that everything can be measured and broken down into smaller and smaller increments. Get out one of those thick measuring tapes with great big numbers on the face (the big type for people whose eyes aren't what they used to be, like me!) and show them: What is an inch? What's a foot? Teachers in classrooms often take this chance to measure all the students and ask them, "Now who is the tallest?" Those types of questions always start little minds working and get them thinking about the world in terms of size, and comparing different sizes (like length, weight, shoe sizes, and more).

Early Learners (6–9) can go a little bit further with that idea, digging into the measurements themselves. Give each child a yardstick or measuring tape and ask them, "How many inches are in a foot? Okay, now how many feet are in a yard? Why, 3, that's right! But now, how many inches are in a yard?" This will help them understand that any measurement unit is made up of other units. Pretty nifty, isn't it?

Terrific Tweens (10–13) can take the ball and run with it, by breaking things down even more. Ask them to divide a foot in half. "Now how many inches is that? Great. That was pretty easy because you can see it right there on the ruler or measuring tape. But how about this: How many feet go into 5 yards? If there are 3 feet in 1 yard, then you could get the answer by multiplying the number of feet by the number of yards (3 x 5 = 15). Is there another way to state that problem? Here's another one: Without looking at a measuring tape, how many inches are in 2 1/2 yards?" Ask the kids how they can figure it out. "What does the problem look like?" Pretty quick, you'll see a light bulb go on over their heads, especially when they come up with a way to figure out the inches in any measurement.

Kids of all ages love building their own SFG box and adding their own details, like this teen's custom vertical trellis.

Cultivating Teens (14+). When you're dealing with teens, start them on the idea of converting. "How many centimeters are in a foot? Is there even a metric equivalent to a foot? How many centimeters is your SFG box? What's the basis for the metric system? Why yes, it's the number 10! Is this better than or just different from the American standard measurement system? Why?" See how far you can take it. You can even turn it into a geography lesson by asking the Teen Cultivator, "What countries currently use the metric system?"

Math Blaster

My first job in life was being an engineer. Engineers use math to solve problems. So it's no surprise that Square Foot Gardening was developed around basic math. That means SFG is just about a perfect, fun, and easy way to learn math. There are so many possible math lessons that I discover new ones all the time.

Preschool Growers (2–5). Use the SFG box to get the youngest gardeners familiar with numbers 1 through 9. Make a large sketch of a 3 x 3 SFG box with 9 squares inside. Then give your child a colored marker and have her draw the number 1 in a corner square. Help her if you need to, but continue adding numbers until all the squares are marked. Have a big group of kids, or even a classroom? Great! Hand out different colors of markers and let the boys and girls take turns filling in the squares' numbers. You can ask for volunteers, "Who knows how to make a '1'?" and so forth. Don't worry if they can't stay in the lines, the important part is getting familiar with their numbers.

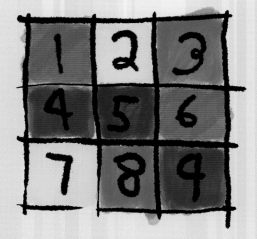

The best math is vibrant math that kids can have fun with. Give your child some sidewalk chalk and have them draw a full-size SFG box on a driveway or blacktop. The child should number each square in order, each in a different color. Now, start a skipping game. Each child jumps into a square and says that number, starting with "1." Then see who can do it backwards, or with one foot in one number and one foot on the other. If they are old enough, see if they can do just even numbers or just odd numbers. Won't that be fun? I bet the kids can come up with their own games using the numbered squares. Just step back, watch, and see! Be ready to applaud their ingenuity.

Early Learners (6–9). Elementary school-aged children will find the SFG box a big help in learning simple addition and subtraction. Here's how you do it: Put a big "1" in the first square, and a "2" in the second square, and ask, "What is 1 plus 2?" The answer goes in the third square. Now put a "4" in the next square. What equals "4"? Yes, 1 plus 3 will do it, but what other numbers might equal 4. How about 2 plus 2? Now the children start to see that there are different ways to arrive at the same answer. You can teach subtraction as well. Ask, "If Billy will plant 3 squares, and Julia plants 3 squares, and there are 9 squares total, how many squares are left for Cindy to plant?" The answer is 9-3= 6 and 6-3 = 3, of course. But the kids will see the equation when they can relate it to actual boxes. See? An SFG box with its 9 squares can be quite a learning tool!

Terrific Tweens (10-13). Older kids already know subtraction and addition, but their SFG boxes can help them learn about multiplication and division. It works the same way—have them draw the box, put in numbers 1 through 9, and then draw lines to show different multiplication or division functions. But how about some division problems? How many rows go into a box of 9 squares? (9 divided by 3). If you have to, you can count the rows to find the number. How about this: If we have 3 children, how many squares will they get to plant? See how many things you can learn from this simple gardening system? Make up some more.

Cultivating Teens (14+). Teenagers are dealing with more complicated math, but the SFG box can help them as well. For instance, which numbers in the box also have their square roots in the box? (The answer is 1, 4, and 9.) You can even introduce complex concepts. What if we have 2 gardeners for the 9 squares? How many squares does each gardener get? We know it's 4.5 squares, but if a teen has difficulty doing that in long division, they can see the problem right in front of them. The two gardeners would each get 4 squares with one square left over. The fair thing would be to divide the leftover square in half. So the total is 4 and 1/2 squares for each gardener, or 4.5, because .5 is half of 1. There are also fractions. What is a fraction that equals .5? How about 1/2? But the best way to get teenagers thinking about math in their SFGs is to have them make up the problem. When they come up with problems related to their homework, they are actually working out the logic in the problems as they do it.

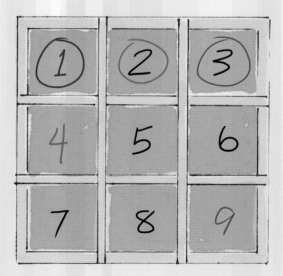

Puzzle Me This

What is the definition of a square? Let's see if your child can come up with a definition of their own. All sides the same length? Yep. All corners are "right" angles? Okay, is there another way to say "right angle?" (How about 90 degrees? Is your child ready for angles and what is 360 degrees?) Let's build on that until we have good definition that will tell us what a square is, and what is not a square. And to go along with that idea, how many actual squares can your child (and you) find inside a 3 x 3 SFG? (The answer is 14.) Draw one out to prove it. How about in an adult-size, 4 x 4 SFG box? (Anyone get 31?) For the very young, you can always start out with that question for a 2 x 2 box. That might be easier for the parent, too.

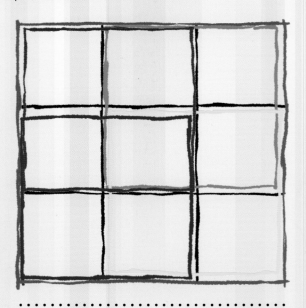

How many squares can you find in a 3 x 3 SFG?

The math lesson might start with box building, but it does not end there. Once the planting starts, the arithmetic really kicks in—but in a very fun way.

Put your box in a high visibility spot, such as near the front door or outside a well-used window so your kids will see it often. Let her personalize the box to increase the feeling of ownership.

Where to Put that Box?

Now that the kids understand all about the SFG box, it's time to pick a place to put it. First, kids need to know that the best location should get six to eight hours of sunlight each day. Let them investigate the yard (and let's not forget that the front yard can be a great place to put a child's SFG box—it's wonderful way for them to show it off to the whole neighborhood!) to see which areas get a lot of shade, or a lot of sun. Let's avoid areas that puddle and don't drain well. So no putting the box in the swimming pool.

We want our box to get plenty of sunlight, but we like to keep the excitement level high by putting it where children can see it from the house, or better yet, right from the bedroom window (or right next to the front door). The more kids actually see their boxes, the more likely they are to check on their SFG, be proud of everything that's growing, and take good care of their plants. The best way to determine where the box will go is to consult the sketch the child made of the yard.

Say What?

Kids who spend enough time in the garden are eventually going to hear the word **photosynthesis**, or they're going to bring it home from school. So let's take a look at that word. Have your child look at it. It is really two words jammed together, isn't it? "Photo" is the first part, and "synthesis" is the second part.

We know what photos are right? They're pictures. But did you know that the word "photo" comes from the Greek word "phos" or "light"? "Synthesis" means to combine different things to makes something else. So if you look at the word again, photosynthesis is how plants use light with other things like soil nutrients and the air, to make a third thing: food. Isn't that wonderful?

Although younger children will just need to know that they have to look for the sunniest spot in the yard, ☙ Early Learners (6-9) can handle more complicated ideas about sunlight and plants. They'll want to talk about how plants use sunlight to make their own food. They might have heard the word *photosynthesis*, but can't really explain it.

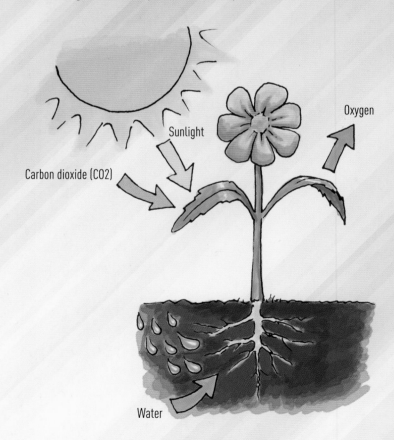

Sunlight

Oxygen

Carbon dioxide (CO2)

Water

Photosynthesis is how most plants make food. Here's how I explain it: Imagine you're shrunk down and inside a plant leaf. You would see bright sunlight coming in, and it would contain energy. That energy combines with the water and minerals from the soil that came up from the roots, and the carbon dioxide coming in from the air, to form a type of sugar. Everybody likes sugar, right? Well so do plants. You would see some sugar flow out into the stems and into the plant's fruits and vegetables and the plant would change some of their sugar into something called starch, which they would store in other parts of the plant for later. Like putting food in the refrigerator. They don't look like they're doing very much, but once you get inside them you can see that plants are very busy aren't they?

☮ Terrific Tweens (10-13) will be able to build on that knowledge, and other things they've learned in school biology and horticulture classes. You can really have some wonderful discussions with a teenager about sunlight and SFG plants—it becomes a science lesson. They are able to grasp that in photosynthesis, special leaf cells called "chloroplasts" use chlorophyll to trap sunlight. The cells then combine the energy from the sunlight with minerals and water from the soil. The process breaks up the water molecules into oxygen—which the plant releases—and hydrogen, which is combined with carbon dioxide molecules taken in from the air to create sugars that the plant can use to grow. Some of these sugars go into growing new leaves, flowers, and fruit, while some are converted to starches for use later. Have your teenager draw a diagram explaining the process of photosynthesis, and you might wind up with something pretty spectacular. No matter what though, we always want to come back to the SFG box, and that box needs to be placed where it will receive six to eight hours of strong sunlight a day. Then their plants will grow as strong and healthy as possible.

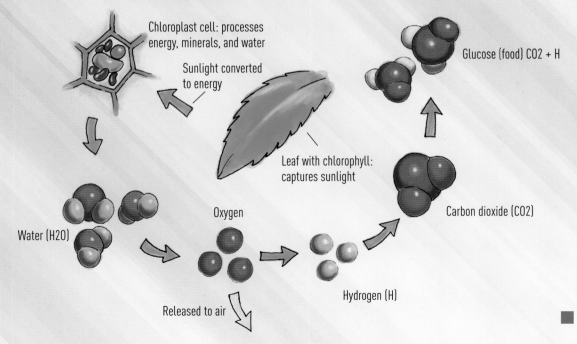

Chloroplast cell: processes energy, minerals, and water

Sunlight converted to energy

Glucose (food) CO2 + H

Leaf with chlorophyll: captures sunlight

Water (H2O)

Oxygen

Carbon dioxide (CO2)

Hydrogen (H)

Released to air

Building Together: Making Your Own SFG Box

2

For most kids, building their own SFG box is the point when the garden physically takes shape. They see up close where all their plants will live and grow. And by building their own box, they learn a little something about independence and achievement. Of course, a lot of kids are just going to be excited because they get to work with tools and build something!

The classic Square Foot Garden box is made from wood, like the nice quality cedar seen here. But there are many other materials you can use if you prefer them or simply because they are on-hand. The only limitation is that the material must not be treated with chemicals or paint or have sharp edges.

Building your SFG box is a great opportunity to teach kids about using power tools (or any other tools) safely.

The Materials

Start the great big SFG box adventure with the materials the child will use to build the box. And, wow, there are a lot of possibilities. They are all possibilities for learning as well.

The SFG box can be built out of just about any material as long as it meets certain restrictions. First and most important: the material cannot contain anything that might contaminate the soil and get into the plants growing there. That means paint or preservatives used to treat wood, or oil-based paints on metal or bricks are no-nos. Even though you can use many different materials, most people choose wood for good reasons. Wood is a natural, replaceable material, it's easy to work with, easy to find, inexpensive, and looks good too.

But the kids should have some ideas about what they want to use, and it's a good chance to discuss building materials.

Start with what an SFG box must be. We want our box to be:

- 3 feet x 3 feet.
- Square.
- 6 inches deep.
- Durable.
- Portable, if we want to move it later.
- Nice to look at.

A wood SFG box kit has all of the parts cut and predrilled for screws in advance. All you need to do is drive four deck screws at each half-lap joint to secure the corners.

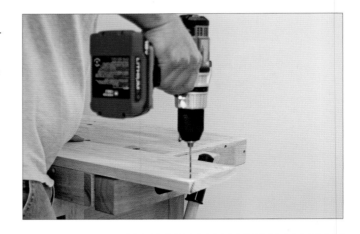

If you are not using a kit, you'll need to predrill pilot holes for all the fasteners to the ends of the boards so they don't split.

Concrete blocks and other masonry products work great for making an SFG box right in place. You don't even need to bond them together with mortar. Just stack them neatly so they make an interior box that is roughly the size you need.

So with all that in mind, let's ask a few questions about what might be the best material for our SFG boxes.

- Why is wood a good choice for the SFG box?
- What other materials could we use?
- What about glass? Could you use glass for the box? Why or why not?
- What about metals? What different types of metals are there? Which would be best for a box and why? Where would we find those metals? What would be some of the challenges in using metals?

- What about bricks or concrete blocks? What would be good or bad about using bricks or concrete blocks?

Let them discuss all the pros and cons about what to use to build their boxes, but generally, wood is going to work best. So the instructions that follow are geared to using wood for a child's box.

Science Discovery

Where does wood come from? That's a pretty easy question that just about every child can answer. But you can leapfrog on that question to really investigate the topic of science and botany.

Ask ⬤ **Preschool Growers** (2–5) if wood can come from any tree. Does the wood keep growing after you cut down the tree? No? Wouldn't it be funny if it did? What would that mean in our houses? (Kid's get a real kick out of fantasy meeting reality, but this is also a fun way for them to understand the basics about wood.)

Investigate with ✿ **Early Learners** (6–9) what makes trees different from other plants. Have the kids make a list with two columns: "the same" on one side, and "different" on the other—they can make it right in their SFG Journal. Start with what is the same. Do trees grow from seeds? Yep. Do they grow straight up? Well, usually. What do they need to grow and where do they get it? How long do they live? And of course, that depends on the type of tree you're talking about. Trees can live anywhere from a few years to hundreds of years. Yes hundreds! And even thousands!

What other ways can you think of that trees are different from the plants in our garden?

Lifespan is just one of the ways trees are different from other plants.

All those ✿ **Terrific Tweens** (10–13) are plenty smart enough to learn about the different types of trees. This can be the perfect chance for a field trip to a forest, a national or state park, or even a very large local park or wildlife preserve. You can call it being the tree detective. Start with a list of discoveries to make. What types are there? Let's start with the two basic types: deciduous (leaf bearing) or coniferous (needle bearing). Do they grow in the same places? Which grows higher? What are the shapes of needle bearing and leaf-bearing trees? Let's get them making a list, taking some pictures, and maybe even drawing some shapes in their SFG Journal.

Challenge ✿ **Cultivating Teens** (14+) to really develop their tree-high smarts. This subject alone could make for a whole class. Ask them to write a quick couple of sentences describing the difference between a hardwood and softwood. Ask them to name three species of each and describe how scientists tell the age of a tree. Now it get's fun, because you can ask them to go out in the forest and look at fallen trees, and figure out the ages.

Deciduous trees have leaves.   Coniferous trees have needles.

Fascinating Factoid

Here's something that's sure to tickle even a teenager's imagination. The oldest tree is more than 4,700 years old (it's called the Methuselah Tree). That sure is old, isn't it?

The box can lead to a bigger discussion about the environment and ecosystem. For instance, you can ask the teenager, "Which is better at taking carbon out of the air, a tree or grass in the same area?" You can discuss how trees help clean the air of carbon dioxide, how important forests are in the ecosystem, how they support diverse species of animals, other plants and important insects, and just how nice they are to spend time around. Wow, there sure is a lot to talk about when it comes to trees.

When I build an SFG box, I like to use wood. Can you guess why? Yes, because it's easy to work with, a nice natural material, and it looks great. But one of the things I like best about wood is that it is easy to find free wood.

SFG ACTIVITY

Hunting for wood for an SFG box is actually a great way for a group of kids, or one child accompanied by an adult, to get out and learn how to socialize. It's this easy: No matter what age your child is, walk around or drive around until you find a big construction site. It can even be a big home remodeling project. Find the person in charge and have your child ask for any leftover wood. You'd be surprised how friendly people are, and how willing construction professionals will be to help out on a child's project. Remember, you're looking for pieces that are least 3 feet long by 6 inches wide, and that have not been used for concrete forms, or treated with preservatives or other chemicals. Imagine how puffed out your little one's chest will be when he or she goes out in the world and comes back with the wood to make their own box.

What About Rocks?

You could try to build a box out of found stones. Depending where you live, you might find a great big field full of round or flat fieldstones (always ask the owner of the field if you can take them!). They can be stacked to create a box.

Flat stones can also be used to build an SFG. Be sure your kids wear gloves when handling heavy stones and blocks.

My favorite kind of wood for building SFG boxes is free wood. For safety, it's very important that an adult supervise their kids before letting them rummage through a stack of scrap wood. Rusty nails and splinters are nothing to fool around with.

Exciting Writing

Let's get kids even more engaged by starting them off with their very own SFG journals. An SFG Journal can be a regular lined-paper journal you buy at the store, a great big sketchpad, or a three-ring binder. I like to tell kids that it's the story of their Square Foot Garden. "You're going to write a book," I say, "and it's going to be all about your SFG!" It gives them a chance to express themselves and record the decisions they make about the garden. Have kids start the Journal with sketches or lists from the planning stage,

and make sure they know they can include anything they want to. A seed packet that caught their eye? Okay, staple it in. A carefully numbered and drawn list of plants? Yup. A story about the first bell pepper they ever picked? You bet. It's all theirs, and it becomes a wonderful reminder of their gardening experience—one both you and your children are bound to cherish. It can also be a great record for future use, if the child makes notes about what did and didn't work in the garden.

SFG Safety Rules

1. We only work with tools when an adult is there to supervise.
2. Children and adults always wear the appropriate safety gear: safety glasses, a dust mask, gloves, and work clothes (including shoes with enclosed toes).
3. Only use tools that are in good condition. No splitting or rotting tool handles, drills with frayed cords, or other poorly maintained tools. Always check that your tools are in proper working order before using them.
4. No working with people who are tired or cranky! You can always come back and do the project after nap time or tomorrow (that includes parents too!).

Putting the Box Together

Now that your child has gathered the materials he or she will need, it's time to get organized and get building that SFG box. If you're like most parents and teachers, you've discovered that kids love nothing better than to work with tools, just like a grown up. So this part of the SFG process is especially fun for the little ones. The engineer in me likes it because it shows children how things go together. If you have ever seen an adult mess up the simple instructions for assembling a bookcase or a kitchen table, you know how important this life skill can be! Let's get started with a few safety rules to make sure this is a happy experience for everyone.

Building a box is a simple job, but whenever you're working with tools and children, the child must be supervised and wearing all required safety gear, including eye protection.

Setting Up a Work Site

Set up your work site as close as possible to where your child's SFG box will ultimately go. The best place is a flat level surface with lots of room to move around. With children, it's always a good idea to make an actual staging area. This can be a driveway, a tarp laid out on the grass, or even a large piece of plywood or cardboard. The idea is to keep tools and materials in one place while you work, because sometimes in all the excitement of building something, youngsters can misplace tools. We wouldn't want Dad losing his favorite screwdriver, would we?

Collect all the materials you'll need for the project and organize them in the staging area. For the wood box we'll be building, you'll need the following:

A hard, flat work surface is the safest site to work on. Good lighting is also important. If you'll be painting the outside of the box your work area should have good ventilation as well.

- 4 boards, 3 feet long x 6 inches wide (should be 1 or 2 inches thick)
- 4 pieces of lath, 3 feet long
- A pencil
- Cordless drill and bits
- 12 deck screws
- 1 roll of landscape fabric (see if you can buy a piece just 3 feet long at a garden center, or a pre-fab SFG box kit usually comes with the weed fabric and grid)

How to Build Your Own Box

Actually building the box is simple once you've collected all the proper tools and materials.

1. Have the child stack the four boards, one on top of the other. Now help them hold one board perpendicular, on it's edge, at the end of the stack. This board is used to mark the overlap width. Mark the width of the board along the ends of each of the other boards.

2. With the boards stacked up and aligned, pull each one out in order and drill three pilot holes for screws, spaced evenly from edge to edge. If you are using 1x wood stock (actual thickness is ¾"), draw a reference line ⅜" from the end of the board to help align your screwholes. For 2x stock (actual thickness 1½") draw the center reference lines ¾" in from the ends. Drill three or four pilot holes at each corner. For standard deck screws, use a drill bit that's about ¹⁄₁₆" diameter.

3. Hold or clamp the boards together, overlapping each successive corner. Drive deck screws into the predrilled holes until the screw heads are just slightly below the surface of the wood.

Option: Add a Box Bottom

Sometimes, a child's SFG box will need to be portable. Maybe it will need to be moved between a schoolyard and home at the end of the school year, or maybe your child will want to take the box with them her when visits grandma and grandpa for a month-long summer vacation. Not to worry; any SFG box can be made portable.

Most kids can easily add a bottom by cutting a piece of $5/8$-inch plywood to match the outside dimensions of the box. Your child may need some help to screw the bottom to the side boards of the box—use a drill with a screwhead bit and 2-inch deck screws. The child will also need to drill a $1/4$-inch drainage hole in the center of every square foot, and an extra one in each corner of the box. The bottom is also necessary if your child wants to place the box on a patio or deck or put it up on an outdoor tabletop.

Sometimes it's okay for kids to have some fun with your tools. Tape measures are always a fascinating item to children. Let them measure things to their hearts content, and try to ask them questions along the way. How tall are you today?

Placing the Box

Now it's time to put the box where it belongs. We want to make sure, however, that no weeds grow up into our box. So what do we do? Work with your child to remove any grass or plant life underneath where the box will go. Then he or she will cut the landscape fabric to fit underneath the box.

This fabric is a special material that will block weeds and other plants from growing up from underneath the box. Remember, we only want the plants we choose to grow in the box! One of the best parts about Square Foot Gardening (and one of the favorite parts for kids) is that an SFG never needs weeding. Never!

So we use landscape fabric as a "floor" for the box. But rather than just tell kids what to do, why not use this as a chance for some creative problem solving and scientific investigation? Ask kids to come up with a list of things that we might use instead of landscape fabric, and figure out whether it will work as a replacement. Remember, whatever we use has to stop plants from growing underneath the box, but it should also allow for water to drain. We don't use or buy "weed cloth" or cheap plastic of any kind because we want something that lasts for 10 years, and we don't like to use plastic in our nice, organic vegetable garden. So what are some other options?

Newspaper. Yes, newspaper is easy to find, cheap, and if you wet it down and use several layers, it could block weeds, couldn't it? It's also easy to lay out under the box because newspapers are the right shape. But let's ask children to think about why it might not work. In science, this is called testing your theory! When they think about it for a little while, most children will realize that newspaper breaks down over time. The box might be weed-free for one season, but next year you might see weeds popping up. Not so good, is it? So it doesn't look like newspaper will be a good substitute.

Cardboard. What about flattened cardboard boxes? They don't cost much (you can usually find free boxes on the curb on the days when people put out their recycling). Cardboard is pretty sturdy, isn't it? But let's keep our scientist hats on. What might be a problem with cardboard? That's right, it breaks down just like newspaper would over time. So cardboard won't do the job either.

As long as they remain interested, work with kids to explore other options. But we've tried lots of different materials over the years, and landscaping fabric seems to be the clear winner.

· ·

Ordinary landscape fabric can be spread out onto the ground to prevent weeds from growing up through the ground and into the SFG box. But because this material is sold in long rolls, you'll have a lot left over. If you have no use for leftover landscape fabric, consider using newspaper or cardboard.

· ·

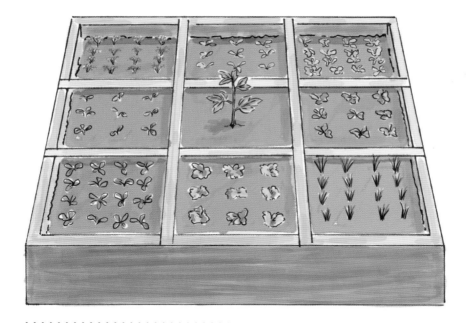

A sturdy grid across the top of your SFG stays in place for ongoing reference as you plant and maintain your garden. Note the groupings of the plants: small (16 per square) in the corners; medium (9 per square) in the middle sections between the corners; and a big (1 per square) in the center.

Making the Grid

Let's take a moment and congratulate the youngster who has just completed their first SFG box. That's a big achievement and a great start. But now we have to build the one thing that makes that box a "Square Foot Garden" box: A grid! It's not a Square Foot Garden without a grid.

That's because the grid helps you space your plants correctly. It helps you when it comes to time to "rotate" crops. The grid lets us know where everything is in the box and is neat to look at as well. But most of all,

making a grid to go on top of the box is a great way to help kids of all ages understand how their Square Foot Garden will work. It can be a real "Aha!" moment for kids and adults alike, when they actually see how the box will be organized, and how each type of plant has it's own, clearly defined square. It's almost like 9 different miniature gardens all placed next to each other, because we plant a different crop in each of the squares, separated by the grid.

So how do we make a grid for our SFG box?

I bet your child can dream up lots of ways to make a grid on top of the box. But we have to be thoughtful about what we use. An SFG grid has to be durable because it will get wet and will spend a lot of time in the hot sun. That's why we don't use string or rope for the grid. Those will eventually rot. Even if they didn't, though, something like string is bound to sag, get dirty, and eventually break. In addition, you have to drive a nail in the sides to tie the string to, and that nail sticks up and will soon get rusty. That's trouble in River City for small, soft delicate hands. So it's better to use something a little stiffer. Most people use wood to make their grid, although I've seen gardeners use aluminum blinds or strips of plastic molding. Just as long as you can see it, it's non-toxic, and it's permanent, it will be okay.

Fortunately, there is a building material called "lath." These thin strips of wood are just about perfect for making a grid. You can find lath at home centers and lumberyards, and this is a good chance to teach kids about shopping and budgeting.

Any children old enough to write should add the price of the lath to what—if any—was spent on the lumber for the sides of the box. Keeping a running tally of expenses in their SFG journals will open their eyes to how quickly the cost of something can add up. We want to make sure kids record the whole "story" of their Square Foot Garden

Wood lath can be found at most building centers in 3-foot lengths and it is so inexpensive it is practically free. You have to pick through it carefully to find pieces that are in good condition throughout their length.

adventure. Help older kids get a good lesson in budgeting by having them add the cost of gas to get to the store, and the time it took for the shopping trip.

SFG ACTIVITY:
Learning to Shop

🔵 Preschool Growers (2-5) and 🟢 Early Learners (6-9) will usually be excited if you tell them, "We're going to buy what we need to finish your Square Foot Garden box." When you get to the store, have the kids ask the store greeter where the lumber is kept. Take the chance to explain to younger children that when you need to find something in a store, ask one of the clerks. Then take the little SFGers to the lumber aisle and have them help you pick out pieces of lath. Now you can let them be big boys and girls by figuring things out. How much do they cost and how many do we need? What's the total cost? Do we have enough money, and how much change should we get back? Is there anything else we need while we are here at the store?

When it comes time to pay, let them hand the money to the clerk and take the change. Just think how big and important they'll feel, and how much you'll be building their confidence.

🟡 Terrific Tweens (10-13) can be more in charge of a shopping trip. Start before you even go to the home center. Ask "How much lath do we need?" They will have to measure the box and figure out that they'll need four pieces long enough to cross the box. Drive them to the store, but tell them that they need to find the lath, and purchase it. This will give them a chance to exercise their independence and really take charge of their SFG.

Do the same thing with younger 🌱 Cultivating Teens (14+) but those teens old enough to drive can go buy lath all on their own. They may even have their own money from babysitting or an afterschool job. Tell them that it is up to them to complete the box and you'll be giving them a lesson in responsibility.

Build Your Own

Making the grid is easy enough for most kids.

1. Have the youngster mark each piece for cutting (measure twice, cut once—another important lesson).

2. Rather than using dad's circular saw or table saw to cut the pieces, have the child cut the pieces with a handsaw. What did we just save for the environment? Yes, the electricity. This will also teach them how to use a simple cross-cut handsaw, rather than dealing with the danger and cost of a power tool.

3. Lay the lath in place across the box (there may be a little measuring here to make sure each square is the same size, in case the inside box measurements aren't exactly the same all around), and help your child drill guide holes slightly larger than the diameter of the bolts being used to join the lath pieces where the pieces cross.

4. Use tiny nuts and bolts or special pins you can find at the lumber store to put in the holes and hold the grid together. We did remember those bolts on the shopping trip, right?

The Lath Alternative

Lath is a good choice for an SFG grid, but it's not the only choice. I bet your youngster can find other options with a quick visit to the local thrift shop. For example, four used yardsticks could serve as a grid. Kids come across all types of things they can use, and it's a good exercise for the imagination. But one of the best grid materials I've seen are old wood, metal, or vinyl venetian blinds. They are usually as cheap as can be, and all your eager gardener needs to do is cut the strings, lay the slats in place, and cut them to length. Then the youngster drills holes at the intersections, as he would with wood slats, and uses a bolt (or better yet, one of the snap fasteners you can find at craft shops and stationary stores) to hold the grid together. Use a nut on the other side of the bolt, and the grid can be removed from the SFG box, folded up, and stored over winter. How's that for handy?

A word of caution though. Any time your youngster makes an SFG grid using light materials, he or she should make sure the grid doesn't blow around on windy days. The child can put a rock at each point the slats cross, or tack or nail the slats to the frame.

(Above) If you use just one fastener per joint, a kid-size SFG grid will have four hinged joints so you can easily fold it up for storage. **(Below)** TIP: Grids will slide around unless you secure them to the sides of the box.

FUN WITH ART:
Those Personal Touches

Have you ever noticed how much kids love to color? Give them a chance to express themselves and they'll just go wild. Well, you can turn the last step of building the child's SFG box into a super art project. When they're finished, every kid will have an SFG box that looks unique, and that the child can be proud of every time they show it to a friend, a grandparent, or anyone else.

The idea behind this project is the same no matter what age the youngster is: Create an individual piece of art out of their own box. How they do it is up to them. That's the joy of art. The only requirement is they have fun and be as creative as possible. (Those are pretty good rules for all of life, aren't they?)

The easiest decoration is painting the outside of the box. Supply non-toxic paint and tell the children that the health of their plants depends on them not getting any paint inside the box. Of course, the preferred art materials may differ from age group to age group. Jill, the **Early Learner**, may say, "I want to use chalk so that I can change my drawings." Mike, the **Cultivating Teen** may want to use stencils on his box. Don't need to stop there. How else can you decorate a box? Challenge your kids to use their imaginations! How about a sign, a flag, a wind chime or windmill, or even a birdhouse? Remember, the grid can be decorated too. I usually paint the grid white, because I like the nice crisp look of it. But kids can paint

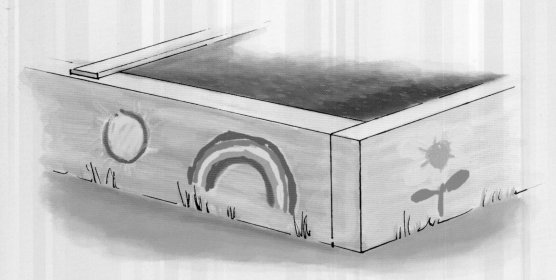

The sides of an SFG box are a little like an artist's canvas—Let your young one's imagination go wild.

it any color. They can even give their friends different colored markers and have them sign the grid. Then that friend will be interested in the garden box and its progress. Wow, think of all the possibilities.

Now your child has a box he or she can be really proud of. Look how much they've accomplished! And think how that box is going to look full of healthy plants. Well, we're almost there. The next step is adding some soil so that the plants your young gardener has chosen have the perfect place to grow big and strong.

A coat of water-based paint on the outside surfaces of the box brightens the garden and gives some individuality to the project. Avoid getting paint on the inside surfaces.

A bright color scheme from the box walls can be carried through to the grid, too.

Getting Dirty: Making Mel's Mix is as Easy as (Mud) Pie

By now, no matter what age your child may be, he or she will start to see that a Square Foot Garden is something special and different. Kids really start to get involved and make sense of things when they've built their own boxes and grids. Now it's time for them to make the soil for the SFG. That's right, we make our own soil.

Square Foot Gardens use a very special soil that we call "Mel's Mix." We are going to make it with three very important ingredients. This soil mix has a perfect combination of nutrients garden plants thrive on, a texture that drains well, and, best of all, a soil with absolutely no weed seeds. You can find bags of pre-made Mel's Mix at some large home centers and nurseries, but for the benefit of the kids, it's better if they mix their own. First though, they need to understand a little bit about what soil is and what it brings to the party.

Mel's Mix is a homemade soil comprised of equal parts compost, peat moss (or coir), and vermiculite—a natural mineral that helps soil retain water and keeps it from becoming compressed and dense.

Corn grown in Mel's Mix

Corn grown in pure compost

The Soil Story

Almost everyone who gets to this point in the SFG process asks, "Why not just dig up your backyard dirt and fill the box?" Which leads us to one of the most important elements of the SFG method. Most gardeners have to improve their garden soil every spring. Why? Because frankly, just about everywhere on the earth, backyard soil won't grow very much except weeds. Kids know that the opposite of fun is weeding, so we don't want weeds in our garden and most kids would prefer not to do the yearly work of "amending" soil with things like fertilizer, compost, peat moss, and vermiculite. Also not fun.

Shawn, an experienced Square Foot Gardener from Minnesota, did an experiment where he planted corn in pure compost right next to seeds from the same batch that are planted in Mel's Mix. Here you can see that the Mel's Mix corn (left photo) is twice as tall as the compost-grown corn (right photo).

My idea, which really appeals to the children I see gardening, is to fill that box we just built with 6 inches of a perfect soil—a special blend we call Mel's Mix—that will ensure kids never have to pull weeds. Now we're on the road to funville. Mix the soil, fill up the box, add a grid, and start a lifetime of happy, successful gardening.

Okay, So What is Mel's Mix?

Mel's Mix is the special soil we make to fill the Square Foot Gardening box. It's a special recipe created just for SFG. Even little children have seen their mom or dad cooking and baking in the kitchen. So it's fun for them to think of making the soil for their SFGs just like mixing up a cake in the kitchen (only they won't have to cook it!). The "recipe" includes three ingredients: *Vermiculite*, *compost*, and *peat moss* (or *coir*). Let's take a look at each of these before we learn how to mix them together.

1. **Vermiculite.** This is a special type of rock. It can be found all around the world. It is dug up and then ground up into small pieces. But here's the neat part—the rock is heated in a big oven until it pops like popcorn! After that, it has nooks and  crannies just like an English muffin. If your child doesn't know what an English muffin is, this is your chance to demonstrate how vermiculite holds water in the soil. Butter a warm English muffin and hold it slightly tilted. Explain that the butter is like water in the soil, and the vermiculite traps some of the water like the muffin's surface traps the butter. That way, even after you water the garden, the soil holds some of the water for the plants to drink.

2. **Compost.** Compost contains lots and lots of nutrients to help garden grow healthy and strong. It also helps soil hold moisture to keep plant roots from getting thirsty, and it has a lot of air pockets that let roots grow free. Doesn't that sound great? The best part is  that compost is created by recycling just about anything that was once growing. We use at least five types mixed together in making Mel's Mix, to make sure that plants get all the nutrients they need.

3. **Peat Moss.** When plant material decays for millions of years, you get peat moss. Now, we dig it up and use it to improve the soil in our garden. It makes the soil lighter, easier to work with, and it acts a little bit like a sponge to hold a certain amount of water, letting any extra drain  right out of the soil. We are now moving to using coir—the fiber from the outside of coconut husks—as a renewable alternative to peat moss.

SFG ACTIVITY:
Get Composting!

You can certainly buy the compost for Mel's Mix at just about any nursery or garden supply center, but kids can get much more involved by making their own compost. If you don't have a compost bin, you can buy an inexpensive model or help your child build a homemade model so your child can learn the art of composting right away. Basically, we can compost just about any plant material or kitchen waste, such as carrot tops, fallen leaves, banana peels, dried grass cuttings, orange peels, apple cores, and even unused lettuce leaves. Children collect kitchen scraps in a small pail kept under the sink (no fats or proteins) and, when the pail is filled, they add the scraps to the compost bin. Get them in the habit of "tending" the compost pile as a lesson in responsibility and discipline. Explain that the materials break down the more the pile is turned and kept moist. They'll be rewarded for their efforts with gardeners' "black gold."

What is in Compost?

Browns

Greens

Good compost requires a blend of organic materials (waste) from around your home and yard. *Browns* (left photo) include leaves, weeds, sticks, wood chips, and even sawdust. *Greens* (right photo) include grass clippings, vegetable scraps, green leaves, and cow manure (note: your dog is not a cow). A ratio of three parts browns to one part greens is recommended.

Math Blaster

How much Mel's Mix do we need? I'm happy to tell you it's very easy to figure out—well, at least for **Terrific Tweens** and **Cultivating Teens**. We have a box that has an area of 3 feet by 3 feet, which equals 9 square feet. (That's using the area formula of width times length.) A square is easy, because the width and the length are equal. Next, we want to find the volume. Volume equals the area times the depth.

Our depth is 6 inches, which equals .5 feet or, in fraction form, ½ of a foot. So look how easy this is. The volume of our kids' SFG box is 3 x 3 = 9 square feet; 9 square feet x .5 foot = 4.5 cubic feet. That's it! You are all done. The next step is to divide 4.5 cubic feet into the 3 equal ingredient parts. That's easy too: each ingredient will be 1.5 cubic feet. Double-check it by going backwards. Engineers always do this as a final check: 1.5 x 3 = 4.5.

Say What?

Here's something neat about the word compost. It is used to describe a thing and an action. That means it's both a *noun*—which is a person, place or thing—and a *verb*—which is an action, or something happening. *Compost* is defined as a mixture of decaying organic substances. These substances can include anything leftover by something that is or was alive. Compost can be made from spent plants and leaves, or even some types of animal poop! It comes from the Latin word *compositum*, which means to arrange various things into a new and better thing.

Where do we Get the Ingredients?

Getting what you need to make your Mel's Mix is going to mean a trip to the garden center inside a home improvement store, or to a big local nursery. That's where you'll find compressed bales of peat moss and large bags of vermiculite. But call ahead to make sure the store has both of those in stock. Every garden center will carry compost. But homemade compost is even better than anything you can buy. So if you have a composter and you've made a good amount of compost, you may already have what you need for Mel's Mix.

Science Discovery

Let's help the kids create their own example of volume and weight. We'll need 6 pieces of cardboard measuring 12 inches by 12 inches. Kids need to find some large cardboard boxes they can cut up into 12-inch squares. The box will then be equal to exactly 1 square foot in area, and we will use it for a special lesson later in the book. Help your child cut 6 squares, each 12 inches by 12 inches. Now they need to tape the squares together to form a box. Once they do that, they've created 1 cubic foot. "Cubic" sounds like cube, doesn't it? There is a cubic foot of air in the box, but what would happen if we filled the box with water? Good, it would be a cubic foot of water. The same is true if we filled the box with compost. They are all 1 cubic foot of whatever it is we are measuring.

Now let's think about the difference. Does water in the box weigh the same as the box full of air? No, of course not. So the weight is different, but the volume is the same.

How do we Measure a Cubic Foot?

Mel's Mix is made of equal amounts of all three ingredients. But those are equal amounts by volume, not weight. Rather than confuse the younger learners with the term *volume*, let's just say, "The same amounts of all three parts of Mel's Mix." They won't really be ready for the concept of volume versus weight. But if you are working with an older child, this is a great chance to teach something valuable about the physics of weights and measures.

Let's start with a simple explanation that kids will understand. *Volume* is a how much space something takes up. *Weight* is how heavy or light something is. The question is, what's the best way we could demonstrate that? See the tip to the left for one good trick.

Mel's Mix Amounts

Now we have to think about measuring our ingredients for Mel's Mix. We want the same amount of each ingredient *by volume*. How do we know the volume? Thank goodness, the manufacturers sometimes put the volume in cubic feet right on the bags of the materials! I say sometimes, because occasionally they put the weight instead of the volume. And to make matters worse, some manufacturers put the volume of their product not in cubic feet, but in quarts! We need to give kids the best shortcuts to buying all the ingredients and mixing them for their own boxes. But there's another way to measure by volume after you get everything home. Remember the box? Instead of a box, we can use a pail to measure out equal amounts of each ingredient by volume.

When kids get to the home center or nursery, let them read the labels and they'll soon discover that none of the ingredients come in 1.5-cubic-foot bags. The peat moss comes in bales marked 2.2 cubic feet for a small bale, which expands to about 4.5 cubic feet, or a large bale marked 3.9 cubic feet that expands to about 8 cubic feet. The vermiculite and compost come in bags of various sizes.

So what to buy? Well, let the kids work it out. They will probably have to buy slightly more than they need. They can always use the extra for a second box if they decide to build another or even help their friends plant an SFG! In any case, the extra materials won't go to waste.

You can skip the math pretty easily if your goal is just to get the right amounts of ingredients for your Mel's Mix. Simply find a large bucket like this 5-gallon plastic bucket and fill it with the same amount of each of the three ingredients. Mix them together and you've got just the right ratio.

Build Your Own

Making compost is sure to save some money, and it a good way to keep trash out of the waste stream, too. If you don't already own a compost bin, you can save even more money by making one yourself, rather than buying one. Explain to the kids that a composter needs to let air get to the decaying scraps, and the child needs to be able to regularly "turn" the compost pile to speed up the decaying process. I bet a young imagination can come up with a way to build one that doesn't cost a darn penny. Let's think about that.

You'll need sides, so what could you use for the sides? How about those wooden pallets they use in warehouses and big stores? You can find those next to dumpsters behind the stores, and they would make handy walls with openings that will let the air in.

How can you connect them? With some wire to tie them together. Leave the front open so that you can get in to turn the compost pile. If you stick four fence posts in the ground, you can wrap the wire around the posts, and tie it to them. Leave the front open and it will be easy as pie to get in to turn the compost every week.

The Special Case of Compost

Shopping for compost is a little different than shopping for the other ingredients. Most companies produce compost from just one thing—like steer manure or mushroom growing. So if we use just one compost in our Square Foot Gardens, it's like feeding your plants just one type of food. They need a full diet just like we do! That's why if you don't have a composter at home, you should buy five different types of compost. Remind your child that the goal is 1.5 cubic feet of compost total. So let's look at the labels closely and be smart about what we buy.

This is a good point for kids to take a break, and write down in the SFG Journal exactly what they've learned about Mel's Mix and the math of volume and weight. Littler gardeners can draw pictures of what they've discovered. Either way, the idea is to keep that journal going, and keep the youngster's interest growing.

Want to rock the fun meter? An alternative to the tarp method (one that can be done with just one person) is to use a big, clean barrel or drum with a tight-fitting lid. The child fills it with the different Mel's Mix ingredients, puts the top on, and then rolls it around the yard. Just be ready for a lot of laughter because there is just something funny about rolling a barrel around the backyard.

Mixing the Mix

When kids garden, they get some naturally fun exercise and time outside (and burn off some of that abundant energy). That's the great part of mixing up a box's worth of Mel's Mix—it's good exercise, satisfying, and fun. It's even easier and more fun with friends or family helping out (you need at least two people to do this). Don't get too rough when you're mixing or you'll crush the delicate vermiculite. If you raise a lot of dust as you work, have the junior gardener mist the ingredients lightly with a spray from the garden hose—just don't get it too wet or it will be too heavy to work with. And if the mixing is creating dust, it's always a good idea for everyone to wear a dust mask.

Don't worry—you don't need all of this stuff to make Mel's Mix, but it is good to let your youngsters figure out which ingredients you need.

SFG ACTIVITY:
Mixing the "Mix"

Tell your child, "You know the mixer in the kitchen? Well, we're going to be our own mixer to mix up a batch of Mel's Mix."

1. Lay out a large tarp on the lawn. Tell your child, "This will be your mixing bowl. Can you imagine a mixing bowl big enough for Mel's Mix? Well of course not. So we need to use a tarp.

2. Spread the different types of compost across one side of the tarp, then top with the peat moss and vermiculite. Measure out equal amounts so that you have about 1.5 cubic feet (it doesn't have to be super precise—we're not baking a cake!).

3. Now, with the help of friends, or Mom and Dad, the youngster pulls one side of the tarp toward the opposite side, folding the ingredients in the process. Now reverse directions to turn the mix over in the opposite direction.

4. If your child has enough friends or family helping, they can pick up the tarp and pour the mix directly into the box. Otherwise, it works just as well to scoop the mix into a wheelbarrow or a bucket and move it into the box in that way.

4 Miracle in a Box: The Thrill of Growing a Garden

Once they start planting their gardens, kids can just sense what's next—picking and eating all those delicious fruits and vegetables. But to get there, we need to get their plants off to a good start. Fortunately, in an SFG, that's no sweat.

As with any type of gardening, your child will either use seeds or transplants, depending on the growing season of the particular plant. But that's where the similarities between planting a traditional garden and a Square Foot Garden end. Remember, we'll be saving seeds and plants because we plant only what we want to grow, no wasting seeds. And we have no thinning—the practice of planting a lot of seeds and then pulling up all that sprout, except one at each spacing for that type of plant.

Whether you are planting seedlings or seeds, it is hard to compete with the excitement of getting your hands in the soil and making things grow.

Planting Gardens with Kids

The Magic of Preschoolers and Spacing

Hi, I'm Victoria Boudman, CEO of the Square Foot Gardening Foundation. I'm also the mother of five gardening children, and I've spent quite a bit of time helping youngsters grow their own Square Foot Gardens. I've come up with some surefire strategies to teach children without them catching on that they're learning something (which is priceless). Here's a little advice for planting an SFG with toddlers and working with very young budding gardeners.

Three- and four-year-old children are just beginning to understand the concept of being a "self" rather than just an attachment to a parent. Most have tiny hands that have not quite grasped the fine motor skills needed to plant little seeds or to draw perfect spacing in the squares. In fact they are just learning to hold crayons and color within the lines. I can't tell you how exciting it is to introduce them to the first thoughts in how a seed grows. They are so quizzical and love to ask questions.

When planting a box with children this little, the best way I have found is to create an event. Read some age-appropriate books about seedlings. Take them to the grocery store with you and pick out veggies in the produce aisle. Teach them the names of the veggies and let them touch the produce. It makes the trip fun and interactive. You don't have to even buy anything. Teach them the colors and let them draw on popsicle sticks pictures of the plants they would like to grow. Some will draw a picture, while others are learning the letters and how to draw the alphabet.

If this box is for the little one alone, I'd recommend you think about making it a 2 x 2 box. Four squares—one for each year of life if you have a four-year-old. It is also easy to count four squares. Have the box ready for them, filled with Mel's Mix (but don't place the grid on it yet).

Show them how you check the soil mix for moisture or wetness. Your Mel's Mix should always be damp to the touch, not completely wet or dry. It's okay for kids to feel the soil, take their trowel or toy shovel, and dig a little. Tell them, and then test by digging a hole to see if the soil is moist all the way down to the bottom. If it isn't, you can get out the hose, turn it to a fine spray, and let them spray over the top. That's fun and if that spray gets someone wet, well, have them pretend they're a flower and it's raining out. Big smiles and waving of arms. We want to show them that it is very important to spray long enough to let the water soak down to the bottom of the box, but it has to be a spray or you will ruin the structure of the Mel's Mix and the plants won't grow as well.

Next step. This is where the grid is unveiled. It is a toy. Hide it behind your back and tease the little one. Make a great show of the presentation and use words like "Ta Da!" Ask, "What do you think these magic sticks are for?" Open the grid and place it on the soil. Show them the little squares.

Tell older kids that we are going to divide one big square into four smaller squares. First draw a line in the soil each way, then lay down the grid in the lines you have drawn. Then take it away and let them do the Zip, Zap. Sing it: "Zip, Zap." It will become a song we all sing under our breath for the rest of our lives. They might as well start the fun right now.

Spacing is a great opportunity to teach more than one child. Say you have a pre-K class and you have all the children sitting cross-legged on the ground next to the box. Ask them to sit knee-to-knee, as close as they can. Then tell them to spread their arms wide. They will giggle and make lots of noise because everyone is touching each other. Then have the class stand up with their arms still apart. Tell them to plant their feet, and that they are now like the seeds they get to plant. Ask if they are happy with how close together and squished they are. Then let them all step away from each other until nobody's outstretched arms are touching. Let them spin around and ask them if they enjoy the freedom and the new space. This is how you teach why we plant our seeds or transplants in a special pattern.

The grid can function as a toy for younger gardeners. Let them play with it all they like before it goes on top of the box and gets to work.

What seeds are good for little fingers?

Bush Beans: Choose from among all kinds of colors. The seeds are big and easy to handle and count. Bush beans are planted 9 to a square. A fun thing to do is have them choose the 9 bean seeds they want to plant, then 9 more just in case. Then have them soak the seeds for 10 minutes in a cup of warm water from the bucket of sun-warmed water you have right next to their box.

Corn: Best to lead children to a short variety. The kids can pick out the number of seeds they will need; we space corn plants 4 per square. Just to make sure, we put 2 seeds in each of the 4 holes we make with our fingers. Show them how corn seeds are all dried up and wrinkled, but if we soak them in warm water for 20 minutes, they will puff up ready to plant for a faster start. If you do that first, while you are talking about their garden box, ask them to count out four seeds then just for good measure four more. Later, once the corn sprouts, if two sprouted in the same hole, we pick the tallest and strongest and snip off the extra one with our pair of children's scissors.

Sunflowers: These beautiful SFG additions grow fast and they make perfect cut flowers. Plant short varieties four to a square, and taller varieties one per square.

Radishes: The best part is they grow so fast the kids will not have to wait long for the seed to become a plant. Plus, you can plant 16 per square. No need to pre-soak these, but children must hold them carefully because they are small and round and roll right out of the hand. Have kids plant 2 seeds in each of the 16 holes they poked with their fingers.

Parents and kids of all ages enjoy the fun and accomplishment of gathering around an SFG box and getting to work.

The squares in your SFG grid give an easy geometry lesson to youngsters as they divide the space for planting by using the "Zip, Zap, Bing, Bing, Bing, Bing" method.

Divide and Conquer!

Let's think back to the first chapter. Remember that we'll be planting 1, 4, 9, or 16 plants per square? Kids need to understand that for their plants to grow as big and strong as possible, they need to be evenly spaced in the square in which they're planted. That's so each plant gets enough food, sunlight, and water. Imagine if a little boy had brothers and sisters who got bigger dinner plates, larger bedrooms, and a lot more room to play. That boy would be sad and grow a whole lot slower than his siblings, right? Well, plants are a lot like people.

But how do we make sure all the plants in the Square Foot Garden get the same amount of space and resources? That's right, we divide up each square into smaller but equal portions for each of the plants that will live in that square. How do you do that though? Yes, you could measure out equal sections, draw it out on a piece of paper, and make sure every plant gets the proper amount of space, but that sure seems a lot of work. Maybe there's an easier way. Yep, there sure is, and we call it Zip, Zap, Bing, Bing, Bing, Bing. All the children need are the fingers of one hand to space any number of plants correctly.

The SFG Toolbox

Children who take a trip to the local garden center or nursery might be amazed at all the tools on sale there. What's even more amazing is that you don't need *any* of them for a child's SFG. Kids can save their allowance for plants and seeds. All they need for their Square Foot Garden is a pencil, a trowel, a bucket, and a pair of child's school scissors. These can all be left outside, right by the box so they are there whenever your child needs them. How's that for handy?

What are they for?

A trowel. For making a hole if you are planting a transplant out of its container or when you are mixing in compost when you replant each square after a harvest.

A pencil. For writing in your garden journal or log. Also if you don't want to get your fingers dirty, for making a hole to plant seeds in.

A pair of scissors (children's size, with round ends). For harvesting some plants like leaf lettuces. Buy these in August when the back-to-school sales are on.

A water bucket. For sun-warmed water. Use a plastic cup to ladle out warm water for each plant.

The only tools you need to plant and maintain a Square Foot Garden are a pencil, a trowel, small pair of scissors, and a bucket.

SFG ACTIVITY: "Zip, Zap, Bing, Bing, Bing, Bing"

Let's start by having your child divide one square neatly into quarters. The youngster just makes a line right down the center of the square with her finger—that's a "Zip" (and it doesn't have to be perfect; remember that we're planting a garden not building a skyscraper!). Then she crosses that line right through its center with a perpendicular line—that's the "Zap." Then she pokes a hole right in the center of each of the little squares she's made—Bing, Bing, Bing (and an extra Bing because there are four quarters). That's where the plants go.

Zip! Use you finger to draw a line in the Mel's Mix bisecting one of the grids.

Above top: Zap! Draw a second line with the finger perpendicular to the first, dividing the grid into quadrants. **Above lower:** Bing, Bing, Bing, Bing! Poke a hole in the center of each quadrant for your seed.

The "Zip, Zap, Bing, Bing, Bing, Bing" System

This is a wonderful way to teach children how to space their Square Foot Garden plants. But more than that, it's a great way to teach them fractions. And it sounds fun to boot! So what is "Zip, Zap, Bing, Bing, Bing, Bing"?

I came up with this as a game to teach children how to quickly divide a square into planting areas, in a way that they would remember and have fun with.

The "Zip, Zap" system works perfectly for planting large vegetables that need a square all to themselves. Draw the Zip line and the Zap line and then "Bing" a hole right in the center where the two lines cross.

Planting small plants? It's easy enough for the child to build on the method for plants that are spaced 16 per square. After the zip, zap that makes four equal quadrants, instead of poking just one hole in the center of each, the child spreads two fingers apart like the peace sign, spaced about the distance between your eyes. Now, in each of the smaller squares, they poke two holes at a time, twice in each of those smaller squares. That will make a total of four per small square. Do that in each of the four smaller squares and you have the magic number of 16!

But what about those plants that are spaced 9 per square? Okay, we can do that.

The child makes "horns" by sticking out the index finger and pinkie, and drags his hand right down the center of the square. Bingo, the square is divided into thirds! Now he does the same thing in the opposite

To divide a grid into nine equal spaces, the child simply spreads his index finger and pinkie as far apart as he can and makes a pair of perpendicular passes through the soil.

direction, making two lines perpendicular to the first two. What does that make? Why, 9 equal boxes! How about that? Now, he just Bing, Bing, Bings into the center of every little box and that's where the seeds will go.

Remember, anyone who doesn't want to get their nails dirty can use their pencil, rather than a finger to make the holes.

When you think about it, "Zip, Zap, Bing, Bing, Bing" is a little bit like playing hopscotch. Can you think of other ways to use games that your kids know and love to introduce new activities?

There's no quicker and easier way to space plants in a Square Foot Garden square than with the Zip, Zap, Bing, Bing, Bing, Bing method. When kids get in the zone, they'll be laughing at how fun this shortcut is. Little will they realize, they'll be in the process of learning math skills.

It should be obvious that even though the Zip, Zap, Bing, Bing, Bing, Bing method is essentially a game, almost like hopscotch with your fingers, the method is great for teaching math ideas and concepts as children play.

I know that you or your child may not be interested in or comfortable with math, and that's fine. You can use the same concepts with denominations of money. This is an example of learning practical concepts through play; we all use money, and it's very tangible, so it can make math concepts even more accessible. We always want to keep SFG fun and engaging for kids, so it's no harm done if you want to skip over any math lessons in garden. We won't tell!

Now the kids get to sow their boxes with their future harvests and learn while they sow. They'll start with what they sow. There are two types of ways to start off new plants, and children need to know how to plant both.

Math Blaster

For ⓞ **Preschool Growers (2-5)** this is a simple way to introduce the idea of basic fractions as they make the holes for their plants. Divide the square in half, and how many halves are there? Good, two. Is there another way to divide the square in half? Right, diagonally. What about quarters? How many quarters are there? They're kind of like half of a half, right? What other type of quarter is there? There is a quarter of money isn't there? What do we call a half of a dollar? Right, a 50-cent piece. But why do we call it a "50-cent piece"? Because another way to think of a dollar is 100 pennies. So half of that is 50 pennies, or 50 cents, right? Good, so now we know why it's called a 50-cent piece.

Any teacher or parent can keep building on these questions and answers to create some dialog about different fractions, different amounts of money, and why things are called what they are called (and other names for those same things).

Build on the process with more complicated questions if you're dealing with older learners. For instance, you can ask them if using one finger divides the square in half, what does using two fingers do? It divides the square into thirds. Now you can talk about how fractions can be written as decimals. As a decimal, the 1 square can be written as "1.0." Remember that ½ is half of the full square. The other way to look at ½ is "1 divided by 2." If you use a calculator (or if you write out long division) you'll see the answer is ".5." And that's a way you can convert all fractions into decimals. For fun, you can have kids write the fractions and decimals in the dirt of the squares as they divide them.

Use numbers instead of coins to quickly illustrate the planting patterns as well as the theory behind the method.

🌱 **Cultivating Teens (14+)** can handle more of a challenge. Let's divide a square into thirds as if you were going to plant nine seeds per square. Now, how do you make ⅓ into a decimal number? Well, like above, you just divide 1 by 3 and, aha! Something different happened, right? We get ".33333" and so on. That's called a *repeating* decimal number, and there are a lot of them.

To illustrate the geometry of the grid, place a dollar in one square, two fifty-cent pieces in another, and four quarters in a third.

Say What?

Kids hear all kinds of words in connection with planting their Square Foot Gardens. It's always helpful for them to know what those words mean, so they can understand what's going on with their seeds and new plants.

Germinate is a funny word isn't it? It's got the word "germ" in it, which doesn't seem very good. You might get sick if you have germs, but this germ really means the first sign of growing life. Some people say, "The germ of an idea," meaning it's just the first start of a bigger idea. That's what a seed is. It's the very start of a plant. And that's why "germinate" is what a seed does, when it begins to grow the plant. Germinate actually means "to develop into an individual." Why not have kids draw a picture showing germination?

Seedling is a word that many children might understand, but it's good to make sure. A seedling isn't the seed, and it isn't the grown-up plant. It is the first growth that pops out of the ground. Seedlings are delicate and need to be cared for so that they can grow big and strong. They are like the little babies of plants, but thankfully they don't need their diapers changed! Some older, bigger seedlings are called "transplants" at nurseries and garden centers, because they are not meant to live their whole lives where they are planted—they are meant to be moved, or "transplanted" into a garden. One other word they use in some parts of the country: instead of transplants, they call them "starts."

When a seed germinates it pokes its head up out of the ground, revealing a thin stalk and usually the seed casing. It is a very exciting moment for young gardeners.

Seedlings are very young plants that have at least one leaf pair on the emerging stem. As they grow and strengthen they will become strong enough to be transplanted into your garden.

Science Discovery

Time to make meteorology fun and help your child make the connection between environment and their garden. Have them dedicate a page in their SFG log to "Outside Temperatures." They'll note the temperature when they get up in the morning, one or two times during the day, and when they go to bed. For *Preschool Growers (2-5)* and *Early Learners (6-9)*, just making a simple chart with one column labeled "Temperatures," and 3 to 4 lines labeled by the time of day, will be enough for them to see the general trend of temperatures—to rise during the day and go down in the afternoon. *Terrific Tweens* and *Cultivating Teens*, on the other hand, can make that chart work a little harder. They can add a line at the bottom called "Average Temperature." Now what's the average daytime temperature? Well, if the kids have noted the temperature at four different times, they can get the average by adding the four numbers in the column and then dividing by four. They've just learned how to calculate averages, which can come in handy when they're following their favorite baseball player's season!

Starting plants from seeds is the most fun, because you get to choose the seed packet you want and then be involved in every stage of the growth from seed to food.

Sowing Seeds

Most of the plants a child chooses for their SFG will be started from seed. Kids get a kick out of handling and sowing seeds; it's a simple challenge that keeps things lively, but easy enough to accomplish so that nobody gets frustrated—all with a great feeling of satisfaction at the end. Seeds have to be planted soon enough and at the right time of the year to be successful. Seeds are usually planted when the temperature outside will stay consistently above 50°F. This is a chance for even young children to practice making a chart.

SFG ACTIVITY: Pinching Seeds

We make practicing planting single seeds into a game, so that kids can perfect their technique without being bored. This is a little like darts, only you play it with the seeds and a sheet of white paper. Have your youngster draw a target on the paper, with smaller concentric circles inside and a bulls-eye at the center. Put it on a table in front of a chair. Now your child pours out just a few seeds from the packet into the palm of one hand, and tries to pinch up one seed with the index finger and thumb of the other hand. Have the child drop the seed on the white paper. Sometimes, they think they picked up just one, and it turns out to be three or four. After a little practice, even **Early Learners** should have no problem with the exercise. Younger children can usually easily plant larger seeds, but you may need to help out with the smaller seeds, to prevent overplanting and waste of seeds.

Pinching seeds is a drill to help kids practice handling seeds before they get out into the garden for real. Spread some seeds on a white piece of paper and see if the child can pick them up one at a time. For extra credit, draw a bullseye on the sheet of paper and see if she can set the seed down on the target.

Pinching Seeds

Once you're sure that the temperature is right for planting (let's have kids check the seed packet, and older kids go online and check frost dates in your zip code and other sites to determine the best planting times for the plants they've chosen), it's time to get the seeds in the ground. But you need to make sure your little one can plant seeds one at a time. This can be more difficult than you might think, depending on the size of the seed.

That's why I suggest even adults practice the SFG "pinch" technique, before actually planting any seeds in the garden.

In the garden, the child first checks the dryness of the Mel's Mix to make sure it is moist before starting the seed planting. Then they tip a few seeds into the palm of one hand, and pinch two to three seeds, placing them in the hole that they made with Zip, Zap, Bing, Bing, Bing, Bing. (The hole should be 2 to 4 times deeper than the size of the seed.) Have your child plant one entire square before moving on to the next square and a new type of seed. Spray water on the squares when the seeds are planted.

What's in a Seed?

Teaching in the garden can start with something as small and simple as a seed. Let's ask the kids how they think their seeds are going to grow. Are they going to shoot up to get to the sun? Yes? So the top of the seed sprouts first? Well that's not really the case, so let's see why.

This explanation can be framed for just about any age child because the idea remains the same. Rather than reaching for the sun, the seed looks to get nutrients, support, and water supplies first. So the first thing the seed does is sprout *feeder* roots downward. As soon as the roots take in minerals and water that can fuel growth, the top sprouts and shoots for the surface. So in fact, it's not about sunlight or an internal clock in the seed. It's all about gravity. The seed needs to gather energy so that the top growth can grow up against the force of gravity.

This time lapse sequence shows what happens when a bean germinates and sprouts. Notice how the roots spread downward first so they can collect enough energy for the stem to head up and out of the ground to find the sunshine.

But let's get back to horticulture and biology. One of the most basic questions you can ask young gardeners is: Do all plants grow from seeds? The answer is, of course, no. **Preschool Growers** and **Early Leraners** will be surprised to discover that. Let's just try to get them familiar with the idea that plants can grow from seeds, things a little bit like seeds, and things not at all like seeds. That's why the world of plants is so darn interesting!

For **Terrific Tweens** and **Cultivating Teens**, we can discuss what those other methods are. Ever heard of a spore? It's like a seed, in that it needs a growing "medium" (like soil), but a spore just has the genetic information for the plant—it doesn't have any food and nutrients stored up for the plant that will grow from

Here's an example of spores that you'll recognize. Unlike seeds, spores have no on-board nutrients to help them get growing, and they are also much tinier and usually wind-borne. Dandelions and most types of mushrooms reproduce with spores.

it. Ask kids if they can come up with some examples of plants that grow from spores?

Plants also grow from a host plant, a grown-up plant that provides everything the new plant will need to grow. One way this happens is with *tubers*. Why not have the kids look up and name three tubers. Now we're learning! New plants can also grow from a *rhizome* or a *stolon*. Some people call them suckers and runners, but that's not totally right (that's why you should always call things by their proper names—especially when writing a school report!). Rhizomes are long, thin growths from a plant's roots that branch out underground; new plants grow from *nodes* along the rhizome. Stolons are like rhizomes, but they grow aboveground, and a new plant grows from the tip where it burrows back down into the soil. (Let's make sure we look up all those new words!) That sure is a lot of knowledge, but it tells you how adaptable plants are. And how smart you can become.

Above left: A stolon is a shoot that grows out above ground from a plant and roots in the ground nearby to start a new plant. **Above right:** A rhizome works much like a stolon, except it spreads out underground and the new plant grows upward from a bump in the rhizome called a node.

Science Discovery

Let's explore yet another neat way to grow a new plant: from a "cutting." A cutting is just as it sounds, a piece of a plant that is cut off and used to grow a whole new plant. Not all plants can be grown from cuttings. But when you can, it's like getting a plant for free.

This is a fun and simple experiment that can be done with all ages—you'll need to adapt it for younger children, helping them more with the chart and the experiment itself.

1. Have your child fill 5 small cups with potting soil and 5 other small glasses with clean water.

2. Help them cut two stems from 5 different plants; each stem should be about the length of drinking straw. Be sure to take cuttings from hardy flowering plants like geraniums and fuchsias, shrubs of any type, and a tomato plant if you have one handy.

3. The child should write down the names of the plants from which cuttings were taken, listing them in their SFG Journal. They need to make two columns, labeling them "Water" and "Soil."

4. Now, the youngster cuts off the bottom leaves of each stem, and plants one of each type in the soil-filled cups, placing the other in the glasses of water.

Take two cuttings from three different plants. Plant one of each type in a jar of water and the other in moist soil. Set them on a windowsill and see which grows faster.

5. Let's check every day for signs of new growth, and mark down which cuttings grow and thrive, and which die. What conclusions can the young scientist gardener draw from your "data"? They can write down these conclusions and think about other experiments to learn more about cuttings and test your conclusions! They may even be able to use this as a project for credit in a science class or to enter into a school science fair.

I bet that given half a chance, every young Square Foot Gardener can sit down and come up with 10 new questions about how plants grow, and how new plants are made. Then they should go find the answers to all those questions. They can teach themselves. All that learning, and it started from a tiny seed!

Saving Extra Seeds

Seed companies put a lot of seeds in each packet because they usually sell to traditional gardeners, who overplant

Leftover seeds can be stored in the back of your refrigerator for the next growing season. Put them in a jar with a lid or a sealable plastic bag and be sure to label the packages.

and then thin the seedlings when they sprout. In Square Foot Gardening, we don't waste seeds—we only use a couple per hole. So your little gardener is bound to have extra seeds left over. Don't throw them out! Have junior fold up the seed packets and put them in a resealable sandwich bag. Or, you can store them in a small jar with a lid. Seal the bag or jar tightly, draw a pretty label (pictures work just as well as words) and put the seeds in the back of the refrigerator for next time. Review with your child what two conditions a seed needs to sprout. Wet and warm is the right answer. So what conditions do we store those seeds in to be sure they don't sprout? Dry and cool, of course!

Planting Transplants

Some plants, like most cabbages, take so long to grow that there just isn't enough time in the season to grow them from seed started outdoors. That means they'll need to be "started" inside while it is still too cold outside to plant. Then when the weather gets warmer, your young gardener will transplant this seedling (or "start" as some people call them) in the garden.

In most cases, you'll be buying transplants from a nursery or garden center. Tell your youngster, "These are baby plants. And just like babies, they need to be handled very carefully." Remove the transplant from its pack, and check to see if it is rootbound.

Say What?

Alert! Another gardening vocabulary word: *Root-bound*. It means that the roots have grown so much inside the container that they can't grow anymore, and they are cramped in the available space.

If the transplant is rootbound, the child will use one of my favorite (and one of the very few) SFG tools: a pair of child's scissors. Have the youngster snip off the excess roots at the bottom, loosen the root ball very slightly, soak the roots in a pail of warm water for just a minute, and then plant the transplant in the hole. Pat the soil around the transplant (not too much—it still needs to be fairly loose) and water the new transplants. Now let little hands make a small, saucer-shaped depression all around the new transplant when you water, and it all goes right down to those thirsty roots. That was simple, wasn't it?

A rootbound plant is a seedling that has been in the container a little too long. The roots need to be loosened up before the plant goes from the container into the ground.

How to Prepare a Rootbound Plant

1. Carefully remove the plant from its container.

2. Cut off the excess roots at the bottom with scissors.

SFG Activity

How about growing our own transplants? It's fun and easy, and gives little gardeners something to do before there's any action out in the garden. Let's get started with a little plastic bowl. (We can teach the value of recycling by having the child reuse a cottage cheese or large yogurt container.)

1. Have your child tap a few holes in the bottom with a sharp nail, and then fill the bowl with vermiculite. Put the container on a saucer, and fill the saucer with warm (not hot) water. Now you can tell younger kids that we're going to see magic! Capillary action will draw the water up through the holes in the bottom. The water will rise against gravity, believe it or not, and will darken the vermiculite on the surface.

2. The child then pinches a seed and places it on the surface, repeating with as many seeds as will be needed to fill the all the spots in that particular square of the garden.

3. The child covers the seeds with a thin layer of vermiculite and places the container in a warm spot in the kitchen. Kids will be full of anticipation as they watch every day for the seeds to sprout.

4. As soon as your child sees the first sprouts, have him move the container to a window ledge that gets lots of sun throughout the day (but not too cold at night—you might have to move it every evening, just like putting a baby to bed). Keep just a little water in the saucer at all times. When the sprout develops its first true leaves, the child should very carefully remove it by holding onto the larger round leaves and loosening the root area with a pencil. They can lift it right out (we like to call this "lifting by its ears"). Replant the little seedling in a prepared planting pack filled with Mel's Mix.

5. When the plant grows big enough to be replanted in the garden, soak it first. Then turn it upside down, spank the bottom, and slip the plant out. Loosen the roots slightly and replant into moist soil. Shade and protect the transplant for a few days until it gets established and growing.

Fun with Art

There are so many opportunities for creativity in Square Foot Gardening, and more pop up all the time. I like to give kids the chance to really dress up their Square Foot Garden box by adding plant markers for each square. The plant markers can be attached to a stick that is stuck right into the square (being careful not to damage any plant roots!). Preschool Growers (2-5) will probably need to limit themselves to drawings, but Early Learners (6-9), Terrific Tweens (10-13), and Cultivating Teens (14+) can all decide if they want to make pictures, use letters, include a combination, or do something totally unique (like a drawing of Bugs Bunny for the carrot square). The trick is to use a material that will stand up to the weather and sun exposure. You could use the plastic lid from a large container of sour cream. Would that work? Why or why not? How about having Mom or Dad cut a pointed end on an extra piece of lath or a paint stir stick (that you can get free from the home center or paint store)? You could paint, print, or draw on that. You can even write or draw on a smooth rock. Maybe you could draw a face saying something like, "Mmmm, carrots?" That would be funny wouldn't it! Let's have our little gardeners open the vault of their imaginations and come up with their own ideas for plant markers. Then let's think about all the artistic ways they can decorate the markers:

Draw with colored or regular pencils. Or with "pastels" or markers.

Paint, using watercolors or non-toxic paints of any type. Can you use nail polish? Well, maybe if it doesn't come anywhere near the Mel's Mix! Here's a hint: older kids might want to research homemade paints, like milk paint.

Trace. Is there a way to trace a design onto your plant marker? How would you do that, and what type of designs could you use?

Scan and use computer programs. Maybe the Terrific Tweens (10-13) and Cultivating Teens (14+) want to use their computers to come up with a wild design. They can scan and play with pictures in a program, and then print them out.

Let's ask kids to come up with unusual designs, and maybe even create a different plant marker for every different square in the box! There's no reason they have to be the same, is there? *Imagine* all the possibilities!

....

Free paint sticks from the hardware store or paint store are fun to decorate and use as plant markers in your SFG.

....

Above: Plastic lids from yogurt containers or other food products can be painted and stapled to popsicle sticks as another fun project for making plant markers. **Left:** Don't forget about the plant markers that come with the seedlings when you buy them. They are full of good information for your kids to read and learn. If you are planting seeds, you can also staple the empty seed package to a popsicle stick as a plant marker. These don't hold up to the elements very well, however.

Watering Wisely

How about we all stand back a couple steps and take a look at your child's newly planted SFG box. Doesn't that look beautiful? Those plants need a little bit of care to grow big and strong, and produce some great-tasting fruits and vegetables. Luckily, taking care of the squares is very little work. But all those plants have to get plenty of water to keep them from drying out. Especially when they're young.

Let's talk about this with the young gardener. Could you use a hose? You could, but that's a lot of work to bring the hose to the box every time you need to water. And the water from the hose might be too strong and it's hard to control where it goes. Besides that, the water from the hose is usually too cold for tender little plants. A sprinkler would spray water where you don't need it, and water would be wasted on the surrounding yard.

But keeping a pail full of water right next to the box would work great. Just drop a small plastic cup in the pail and you'll always be ready to water when needed. The sun will warm the water and children can give their plants a little drink of water right at their roots. Remember that saucer-shaped depression the child made around the plant stem? Now they'll see the advantage of that. It's just part of the entire SFG system where all the pieces fit together, just like a jigsaw puzzle showing a perfect looking garden that is more efficient and less work, but more fun!

Keep a bucket of water with a plastic cup right next to your SFG so you can give the plants a drink anytime they need it.

Like anyone else, a young plant needs a nice drink of water from time to time to thrive.

Watering plants this way is no work at all. Most kids find it kind of fun. We call this nurturing our plants—getting up close to them. And, as a little bit of bonus, when they harvest a strawberry or pull a radish up, they can just wash it off in the water and pop it in their mouths! That's about as fresh as you can get!

If you happen to have a family Square Foot Garden, I'd post one of these buckets at every box, so that you make sure no plant will ever go thirsty.

. . . .

Above left: Here's a great tip. You've already got a perfectly good bucket of water right next to your SFG. So what do you do when your hands get dirty? Scrub them right at the bucket. Make sure you don't have anything other than plain soil (Mel's Mix counts) on your hands and scrub and rinse away. The dirt will settle down to the bottom of the bucket so you don't need to clean it that often. And plants love dirt. **Below left:** Pour small amounts of water from your bucket right at the base of each plant. This is the most efficient way possible to keep your garden well-watered.

. . . .

No Maintenance Means No Maintenance

Kids will be happy to find out that watering is about the only thing they'll need to do to keep their Square Foot Gardens growing strong.

Weeding? What weeding? Hey, kids, do you see any weeds? No you don't. That's because we control the soil. Remember how we mixed our Mel's Mix precisely so that we could give our plants exactly what they needed? Well, we didn't mix in any weed seeds, did we? So it's very rare that a weed ever grows in an SFG. And if one does, we just pluck it out roots and all. It's easy because Mel's Mix stays loose and *friable* when nobody walks on it.

What will the kids do with all that extra time? I guess they'll just have to spend it enjoying their Square Foot Gardening and making up games to play around the box.

Dear SFG Journal

Time to make another entry in the journal. When your little gardener is done planting the entire SFG box, they should make a chart of all the plants in the squares. Help the littlest gardeners draw a box and squares, and then they can paste pictures of what they've planted in the correct squares. After the harvest is in, the youngsters can refer back to this chart to see what worked for them, and what they might like to try differently the next time. This is also a really good time to remind them that we add a handful of your best homemade (I hope) compost to mix in that square. They can replant that square with a different crop (go to page 124 to find out why and how) according to the weather and time of year. It's also a good time to have them list their choice of crops for the coming season and, more importantly, what not to plant in that season. Like cool-weather crops versus warm-weather crops, or root crops versus leaf crops versus fruiting crops. It's all so natural and simple. To encourage them to understand succession planting and crop rotation, tell them that Mother Nature does exactly the same thing. She doesn't grow tomatoes (a fruiting, warm-weather crop) if winter is coming.

· ·

Opposite: Now your kid-size SFG is really starting to take shape. By planting a mix of seedling or small plants, like these marigolds, and plants from seed you get a great one-two punch of instant gratification and anticipation.

· ·

Support and Protection

Some of the plants that are children's favorites often need a little help standing up, especially if they get tall before their time or if the area you live in is fairly windy. We want to be a friend to our plants, and friends help their friends out, right? So we should give some support to the taller, lankier plants in our SFGs.

We can do that by "staking" them the single-row way: adding a pole or stick alongside each plant and tying the plant to the pole for support. But that can be quite a bit of work and I found out that if the plant gets too tall before you get around to staking or tying it, a strong wind or rain storm will blow down the plant when you least want it to. So a better way is to use horizontal netting so that any plant taller than 12 inches will automatically grow right through the netting and be supported. All you need is a stake in each box corner. Tie the horizontal layer of netting to the 4 stakes. The netting has big 6-inch square openings. Hey that's a square shape, fancy that! No more tying up every plant and branch. As the plants grow up through the layer of netting, they support themselves. We do that for tall sunflowers, corn, and giant dahlias by installing taller stakes in each corner and adding a layer of netting every foot or so in height. The stakes and netting are reusable.

Other Kinds of Trellises

A tripod trellis is a classic design that can be used anywhere, including an SFG. There are many ways to join the three legs together at the top. A screw eye is used here, but you can make it a little simpler just by wrapping with wire. Unless you make a tiny tripod, the feet will have to rest in neighboring grid spaces, however.

Top left: This trellis is designed just for an SFG box. You'll see how to make it on the next pages. **Lower left:** A trellis made by lashing bamboo canes together looks very exotic and is easy to customize for your SFG box. Use waxed lashing twine to bind the individual canes together. **Lower right:** A trellis made from bent sticks is a fun project to make and it will dress up any SFG box it goes into. For best results, use green (freshly cut) branches and sticks to make a trellis like this.

BUILD YOUR OWN:
Horizontal Trellis Net

Building a horizontal trellis net is a nice activity to keep kids busy and interested, and develop their measuring and construction skills. Because it requires tool use, you should provide adult supervision.

1. The first thing we'll need is some nylon trellis netting. Don't use plastic, it can cut into the plants. Nylon netting is nice and soft, so that plants won't be hurt when they rub against it as they grow and move. You can find this netting at nurseries and in the garden sections of large home centers or on the SFG website. But first, we have to figure out how much we need. How can we do that? Right, we have to measure the area we will be covering. Luckily, in this case, we already know the area: it's the same size as the box itself. So, we need netting 3 feet by 3 feet square. (You can also put up netting over just one or two squares where the tall plants grow, but for our purposes, we'll put it over the whole box.) If the netting isn't sold in just the right size, you'll need to buy the next size up and cut it down to the right size.

2. Next, let's use our trusty scissors to cut the netting to fit over the box. We can just roll out the netting along one side of the box, and then cut along the line of the outside row to make the perfect piece of netting to go over the box.

Above top: Positioning a nylon net a couple of feet above your SFG gives your taller plants good support that they can all share. **Above bottom:** All the parts you'll need to make this horizontal trellis. They include nylon netting and 4-ft.-long pieces of ½˝ EMT conduit. Some nylon cable ties are also useful. For tools, you need scissors and a mallet for driving the support pipes into the ground. You'll also need a hack saw if you have to cut the conduit to length.

Once you have driven a post at each corner and cut and stretched the netting to fit, secure it to the posts about 18 to 24" above the top of the box. TIP: Use nylon cable ties to help keep the netting from slipping down the post.

3. Let's support the horizontal netting with metal conduit. These can be found in 4-foot lengths at home centers. Another possibility is 1-inch by 4-foot long wood posts you can find at lumberyards, or fence posts. Any of the options can be pounded right into the ground at each corner of the box.

4. The netting is simply stretched to each corner and then tied to the pole at that corner. The netting should be at least 1 foot above the surface of the Mel's Mix, with another layer at 2 or 3 feet above, to support the plants just when they start to become top heavy. Of course, if your young gardener has what they think is a better idea, it's always great to let him or her try it out.

We humans are not the only species that enjoys a meal of delicious vegetables. Depending on where you live, it may be a good idea to build a protective cage around your SFG so the bunnies and deer don't get at your produce before you do.

Protecting the Garden

Here's a word that every gardener needs to know: *predator*. Does anybody know what predator means? Find a dictionary or look it up online. You'll find that it comes from the Latiñ word *praeda*, meaning "to plunder." Okay, so what does "plunder" mean? Well, it means to "rob." That means that garden predators rob plants of their leaves, fruits, and other parts. We don't want that, do we?

We need to protect our Square Foot Garden from predators!

Thank goodness that most garden insects don't bother a Square Foot Garden. By making our own soil, we make sure that there aren't any insects or diseases waiting in the soil for the plants to sprout. We also make it difficult for insects, by planting different plants in every square, because there's no one big meal for the pests. That's called *selective planting*, just one of the many built-in advantages of SFG. So fighting off pests usually means just picking the occasional "predator" off a leaf or a stem.

But larger animals can be a problem. They just love Square Foot Gardens. Let's ask the kids what kind of animals might want to have dinner in the Square Foot Garden. What about bears? Are bears a problem? Probably not too much unless you live deep in the forest. Okay, what about tigers? No? Why not? Is it because of where tigers live? Let's figure out where they live, so that we can be sure we don't have any in our neighborhood. The library has books for young and old children about tigers. Or we can do some research online.

Say What?

Any time you're talking about the pests that can bother an SFG, you'll find a lot of good SFG vocabulary words. Like the word for where animals can be found and where they prefer to live. This is important so that you know which animals you have to protect your Square Foot Garden from. Do you know that word? It's *habitat*. Habitat is where an animal normally lives, but most animals can't really survive outside their own habitat. That's why we don't have to worry about tigers getting in our gardens.

But there's another reason tigers don't bother gardens. Can you guess it? It's because tigers are *carnivores*! What do you think that means? It comes from two Latin words: *carni*, which means "flesh," and *vorus*, which means "to eat." So now do you know what a carnivore is? Right! It's an animal that eats the meat of other animals. We don't grow animals in our SFGs, so we don't really have to worry about carnivores, do we?

I bet there's a word for the animals we do have to worry about. Yep, it's *herbivore*. An herbivore is an animal that eats plants. Uh oh, we better watch out for herbivores because there are a lot of delicious plants in a garden. But it's not just herbivores we have to worry about. Did you know that some animals eat both plants and animals? Why there's one of those animals living in your bedroom right now. Yep, it's you. That's because most humans are *omnivores*, or animals that eat both plants and animals. There sure are a lot of words to think about when you're protecting your SFG!

Above top: A tiger is a carnivore, which means it only eats meat. So even if they did live outside of the faraway jungles we wouldn't have to worry about them raiding our gardens. **Above lower:** Deer are herbivores, which mean they eat vegetables. They're also as common as mice in many places. They'd like nothing better than to be invited to your SFG for a good snack.

So we know we don't have to worry about bears and tigers, but what kind of animals do we have to protect our Square Foot Gardens from? Deer? You bet, that's a good one. Deer just love anything that grows in the garden. Raccoons? Yes, they like garden vegetables and fruits as well. In fact, they'll eat just about anything, including garbage! What about birds? They're pretty and they sound nice, but they love some of what you might be growing in your SFG, like corn or even strawberries. Squirrels and chipmunks? They like some things, but they aren't usually much of a problem for a vegetable garden. But what about the burrowing animals, like moles and gophers? No? You're right. Burrowers like to stay below the surface, so they aren't going to bother a raised SFG box, especially since we put down landscaping fabric (or a solid bottom if you made your box portable) that will block them.

How about rabbits, skunks, woodchucks, and possums? It all depends if your house is near their *habitat*. What about house pets? Don't dogs love to dig in dirt? And don't cats sometimes think the garden is like their own litter box? I think we might have to keep an eye on those house pets too.

Deer will think the veggies in your SFG are fine dining.

BUILD YOUR OWN: Wire Cage

Building a wire cage is easy, but requires fine motor skills that may be beyond the ability of **Preschool Growers (2-5)** and some **Early Learners (6-9).** I'd suggest you try to involve them as much as possible though, and talk them through the process so that they get the benefit of understanding how something like this wire cage is built. Older kids will be able to participate more directly in the construction process. Some **Cultivating Teens (14+)** may be able to do it all themselves, for a real feeling of independence. Here's the process you'll use.

This wire cage is made to fit an adult-size SFG, but you'll make it the same way for a 3 x 3 kid size.

1. Gather the materials. You'll need four 1 x 2 boards, 3 feet long (this is a good chance for children to practice their measuring skills, and older children can cut the boards to length with a handsaw); 1 roll of chicken wire with 1-inch openings (these are sold in rolls 3 feet wide, 20 or 30 feet long); plastic pull ties; wire cutting shears or wire cutters; a cordless power drill and bits; staple gun and staples; sturdy work gloves; and 8 deck screws.

What we need is something that would stop the animals from getting to the plants. The plants need to get plenty of air and sunlight, and we want to be able to work with the plants and water them when they get thirsty, right? So we need something that we could take off and put on whenever we wanted to, and that would let light and air get to the plants all the time, while still stopping any hungry critters from making a meal out of our SFG. What about a wire cover? That might do the trick. A wire cover would be just about perfect, wouldn't it? That sounds like an SFG project!

Continued on next page

2. Stack the boards. Stack them as you did in building the SFG box, mark the ends in the same way, and stick each one out in turn to drill the pilot holes for the screws that will hold the frame together.

3. Assemble the frame. Screw the frame together with 2 coarse-thread deck screws at each corner. Overlap the corners as you did with the corners of the SFG box.

4. Roll out the chicken wire. You want to leave enough wire for the sides, so that the cage allows for the mature growth of the plants. Ask your youngster how you might figure this out. Work with him or her to calculate how high the biggest plants in the SFG will grow, then how to make the sides high enough to account for this growth. Usually that is about 3 feet high, so we want to cut a 3-foot wide by 9-foot long piece that goes up one side, across the top, and down the opposite side, all in one piece. We are going to cut two of those 9-foot long pieces.

⚠ Safety First

Cutting chicken wire can be a bit difficult and it can leave sharp edges. Always use thick work gloves when handling chicken wire. It's also smart to cover cut ends with masking tape (or tickle the kids' fancy by letting them pick out a colored duct tape). If you want to play it even safer, have the hardware store or nursery cut the lengths of chicken wire for you.

By the time young gardeners have created protection for their SFG boxes, they have learned quite a few lessons—not the least of which is the responsibility of taking care of growing, living things. That's pretty valuable stuff to know, and there's a lot more to come. Because once that garden is protected and watered regularly, it will grow like nobody's business. That means the next step is harvesting, and harvesting means fun in the garden and treats for little tummies!

5. Lay one 9-foot long piece of chicken wire fencing on the ground and place the frame on top of it. Brace the wood frame with your foot, and bend the chicken wire straight up on both sides over the edge of the frame in a U shape. Then do the same thing with the other 9-foot-long piece.

6. Place one U-shape over the other, perpendicular to it. Ensure that the edges and corners are tight together. Close the seams with plastic ties, attached every few inches.

7. Place the finished cage over the frame and staple it to the frame.

5 The Reward

There is nothing quite like the look on a child's face when she picks the very first tomato she's ever grown. It's plump and red, and sure to be juicy, and it's all hers. That pure joy is what makes harvesting the Square Foot Garden a favorite time for me, and for all the children who have put in the effort and grown their very own SFGs. All their work is paying off (even if it was more like play than work)!

As the garden matures, there are many chances to teach children how to get the most out of their plants. They'll also need to learn when a fruit or vegetable is ripe, and how best to harvest crops without damaging the plants. Of course, older kids can learn ways to get even more out of their Square Foot Gardens, with crop rotation and vertical gardening. So let's learn how to make the most of those gardens!

Harvest time is probably the most special time of year for gardeners. And for first-time Square Foot Gardeners, the thrill of simply looking at and holding the produce you grew yourself is a wonderful experience.

Going, and Growing, Vertical

One of the many benefits of an SFG is that it takes up only 20 percent of the space of a traditional row garden. We save even more space because we grow plants vertically up a support—even plants that are not usually grown vertically, like tomatoes. Let's start our vertical gardening efforts off by asking children what the benefits might be of growing something vertically, up a support.

You can see it better? Well, that's one benefit. What are some others? That's right, air can get to the plants and circulate around them better. The more air circulation around plants, the less chance they have of coming down with a disease, and the fewer places there are for insect pests to hide. A plant growing vertically will also get a lot more sunshine on all its leaves than one growing along the ground or in bush form. And the most important thing of all is that plants have almost unlimited room to grow up. They won't crowd the square they're in, because they are busy climbing the vertical support, and we can make that support as tall as we need.

So vertical growing can be a great way to grow some plants. I say *some* plants, because there are plants we can't grow up a support. Can you think of those plants? Of course, radishes, carrots and potatoes all grow down into the soil, so they couldn't very well grow up a support, now could they? But a lot of other plants will grow wonderfully up a support.

Helping your plants grow upward increases your garden yield without enlarging your garden footprint.

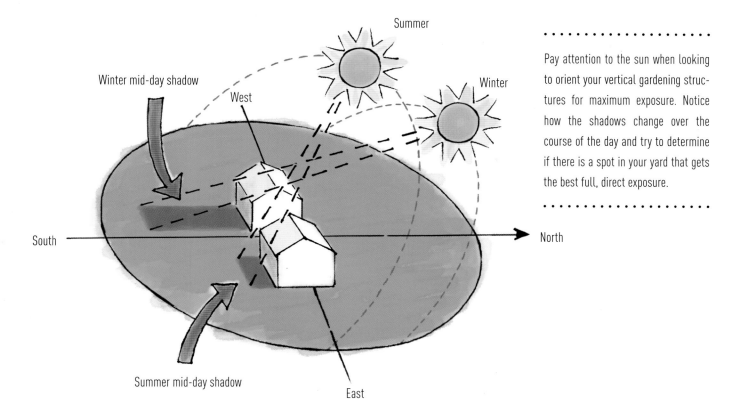

Summer

Winter mid-day shadow

West

Winter

South

North

Summer mid-day shadow

East

To begin with, let's think about where it would be best to put the vertical support on the SFG box. What do we have to consider? Sunlight? That's a good one. Let's think back to when we discussed sunlight exposure. Who knows what direction the sun comes up in each day? Preschool Growers (2–5) might not be able to understand the directions of the sun's movement, so we usually discuss that the sun comes up in the same place every day, and goes down in the same place every night. We have the little ones stand in their yard and face

the direction the sun comes up. This can be very funny, because if there is more than one child, they might all face in different directions. But we point them east, and say, "That's where the sun comes up, every day." Then we turn them to the west and say, "And that's where it goes down every night. Remember how you can see the sunset? That's the sun going down." Help your child become oriented by the position of the house, or their swing set, or another familiar marker, so that they know east and west even if they don't call the directions by their names.

Science Discovery

Here's another important question: If we know that sun rises in the east, is it stronger in one direction or another? If your child has his or her thinking cap on, a little hand shot up and a little voice said, "South." But why is that?

We can actually see why, with a flashlight and a basketball. In a dark room, hold the flashlight on the basketball, as your child holds and turns the basketball just like the Earth spins. It's easy to see that that as the ball turns, the fatter center of the ball is closer to the light, and receives a stronger light because of that. Now we see how the Sun relates to the motion of the Earth. So as it rises and sets, the sun must be stronger in the southern part of the sky!

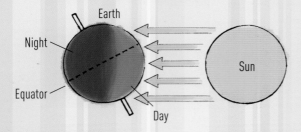

Because the Earth's axis is tilted slightly, sunshine strikes North America at an angle. Because of this fact, light from the south is stronger and gardens that have good southern exposure benefit more from sunlight.

Okay, that's a lot of good information. But let's get back to the original question—which side of the box is best for the vertical support? We don't want the vertical support shading the rest of the garden, do we? So we need to place the support on the north side of the box (or on the side of the box facing a wall of the house, because that's going to block the light anyway)! That's some great thinking through the problem. Now that we know where to put the support, let's build it.

Older Early Learners, Terrific Tweens, and even Cultivating Teens can use their study of the sun's patterns in your yard to explore geography and a bit of astronomy as well. Let's start with the old saw, "The sun rises in the east and sets in the west." Is that always true? Yes? Why? If you said because the Earth spins on an *axis*, you were right. That means the Earth spins like a basketball on the point of your finger. The Earth always spins in the same direction. Now, because it always spins in the same direction, does the sun always come up in the same direction? Right, it does! So what did we learn? The sun doesn't really rise, does it? The Earth is just spinning, making the sun seem like it's rising and moving across the sky.

BUILD YOUR OWN:
Vertical Trellis

I experimented for many years to find just the right material for the vertical support for a Square Foot Garden, and I've worked out these directions to make them easy enough for a child to follow and find rewarding and engaging. For this project we don't want to use wood; it rots and splits. And do not use PVC pipe; it sags and bends. The frame needs to be very strong because wind and the weight of growing plants can put a lot of stress on the frame. Metal makes a sturdy frame, so that's why we use what is known as "electrical conduit" (steel pipe that electricians run wires through) and *rebar* posts to hold the conduit securely in place. Rebar is a special type of metal bar used in concrete construction and it is very strong. Let's start with a shopping trip to the home center. Have your child bring along their SFG Journal to keep track of any money spent and what was bought.

We've tried lots of trellis types over the years, but for vertical gardening with an SFG nothing works as well as our trusted trellis net suspended from a conduit frame.

1. Pick up the materials. Your child will need two 4-to-5-foot sections and one 3-foot section of 1/2-inch electrical conduit (EMT) and two 90-degree elbow connectors from the electrical department. The conduit comes in 10-foot lengths. You can measure and cut the conduit with a tube cutter or hack saw, but most home centers will cut this for you. You will also need two 18-inch pieces of 1/2-inch (no. 4) rebar and a 3-foot wide by 5-foot long section of trellis netting.

2. Assemble the conduit frame. Without tightening the setscrews, add the elbows to either end of the 3-foot section and then attach the other ends of the elbows to one end of each of the 4-to-5-foot sections. Make sure the legs are parallel and then tighten the elbow set screws to the 3-foot section.

3. Drive the pieces of rebar into the ground a fraction of an inch away from the SFG box on both sides of the north end. This is a good chance for a parent to show his confidence in the child's ability to use a mallet with some accuracy by holding the rebar piece for her. However, in some cases it probably makes more sense to start the rebar and let the kid finish driving it. Your call. Don't drive the rebar past the top of the box.

5. Now we need to attach the netting. First, tie the netting onto the two top corners (all but the smallest little ones can do this while standing on a short stepladder). Now cut the netting at each connection, leaving one long strand. Loop each strand over the top of the frame and tie it in a knot. (This is a wonderful way to teach children how to tie knots.) Make sure you keep each strand the same length so that your netting isn't crooked.

4. Slip the bottom ends of the trellis legs over the tops of the rebar. You may have to wriggle the assembly just a little before it slides all the way to the ground. Adjust as necessary so the cross-piece is level.

6. Cut the connections down each side, and repeat the process, tying the sides of the netting to the frame. Tie them nice and tight and they'll stay in place for years. Make sure the netting is straight across at every horizontal string so it looks good. Have the child feel the net-ting and discuss how it's both firm and flexible, and how this allows for plants to grow and bend, but still be supported.

Helping Plants Grow Up

We have to take some extra steps when helping our plants grow up a trellis or support like the one we've built. It's great if kids get in a habit of, once a week, weaving the tops of plants through the netting. You'll want to help younger children with this, because the stems of some plants may be more fragile than others, and we don't want to break off any growing stems.

Let's teach children that some plants, like pole beans and cucumbers, are natural climbers and will climb up the trellis all by themselves. Others, like tomatoes, need to be "trained." Here's another thing we need to do when growing certain plants up a vertical support—pruning.

Say What?

Here's a valuable word for kids to learn: *Pruning*. Pruning doesn't have anything to do with prunes, even though it sure sounds like it, doesn't it? Actually, pruning is something we do quite a bit in Square Foot Gardening. It means to remove any growth on the plant that you don't want. Sometimes, this means cutting off growth that crowds other plants. But a lot of times, it's about helping the plant use its energy to grow up, rather than out. When you "prune" one branch or stem of a plant, the plant will put more energy into the other stem(s) or branches. That's neat, isn't it?

When you are practicing vertical gardening, you need to prune some of the sideways growth from your plants so they can concentrate on moving up in the world.

Some plants want to get bushy and grow sideways, but for vertical gardening we want them to grow up the vertical support. So how can we convince them to grow up, rather than out? The best way is to cut off, or prune, any branches or stems that grow out the sides. A tomato plant is the best example of this. We call the side growth on a tomato plant the "suckers," and we cut them off so that the plant will use its energy to grow up and grow more delicious tomatoes. But you don't need to throw away the suckers—they can become new tomato plants that you can give to friends or family! Stand the suckers cut side down in a glass of water, and when roots sprout, it's ready to plant. Simple as that.

I like to get kids thinking about the space the plants will take up on the vertical support, so no one plant crowds out the others. Tell the little ones, "Remember how we conserve space in our Square Foot Gardens? Well, we have to make sure all the plants on the vertical support have enough room to grow and be happy." So let's give the kids a general rule of thumb. Each plant should spread out no more than 1 foot wide on the support. Have your child grab a measuring tape so that she can see what a 1-foot spread would be on the support. Kids can even mark the netting with non-toxic paint or colored duct tape, to show 1-foot increments across the width of the support. (I bet you can even make a cool art project out of that process.)

As with tomato plants, we like to cut off the side branches or suckers on melons, cucumbers, and squash when we grow them up the support. Let's give squash a little extra room because its leaves are so big—2 feet for that plant.

Happy Harvests

Learning when to harvest is an opportunity for children to work with a calendar and understand months and seasons better. Let's start by what's on a seed packet. When the junior Square Foot Gardener first plants his or her garden, it's wise to note the "time to harvest" listed on the seed packs. Have your child mark a calendar with the dates that their crops will be ready. Preschool Growers and Early Learners may need to actually count days. It's a good time to bring back an old pneumonic device to teach children the different number of days in each month of the year.

> "Thirty days hath September,
> April, June, and November.
> Thirty-one, have all the rest
> Except as February can attest,
> It has twenty-eight days clear,
> And twenty-nine in each leap year."

You'd be surprised that even young children can learn a rhyme like that. Explain that it is a way to remember the number of days in each month, no matter what months they need to count.

Terrific Tweens and Cultivating Teens will be able to calculate the days to harvest much more quickly, and rather than marking a physical calendar, they may want to set an alert on their computer or phone calendar.

When your child plants his or her Square Foot Garden, make a point of reading the matures-in time on the seed package. Calculate what date that means the plant will be ready. Have the kid mark the date on his or her calendar.

It's important to stress to children that becoming familiar with their plants is as important as marking time, because plants may ripen slower or faster depending on local conditions. For instance, if the summer where you live is a bit cooler and more overcast than normal, some fruits and vegetables will take longer to ripen. Here are some specifics about several SFG favorites:

- **Zucchini.** You know they are ripe when they have a nice green color and are 4 to 6 inches long. Let's use our scissors to cut the fruit free from the stem. A child can damage the fruit or the plant if he just pulls it off. You have to pay close attention to zucchini—in just a couple of days they can grow from the size of a nice carrot to the size of a fire hydrant.
- **Cucumbers.** Better to pick early than too late, because cucumbers left on the vine can become bitter. Kids should use their SFG scissors and cut the cucumber off the vine, leaving a small piece of stem attached to the cucumber.
- **Corn.** Corn can be tricky for kids to know when to pick. Let them know that the ear is ready to be harvested when it's completely filled out with kernels. The end will become rounded rather than pointy. The "silk" at the end will start to brown where it goes into the ear. Have your child hold the stalk firmly in one hand (or do this yourself for younger children), and use the other hand to pull the ear down and away from the stalk, twisting a bit to ensure a clean break.
- **Radishes.** Any child can just pull up a radish when it's ready. What's even better is that the young gardener can wash off the vegetable in their bucket of sun-warmed water, and eat the radish right then and there!
- **Carrots.** You really can't go wrong in pulling up your carrot. If you're too early, it will just be smaller than normal, but it will still taste just fine.
- **Leaf lettuce.** The wonderful thing about leaf lettuces is that your child can regularly harvest them, cutting off a few of the large outer leaves for a salad on a regular basis.
- **Cabbage.** Have your child gently squeeze the growing head of cabbage, so that they know when the cabbage ripens and feels solid and firm. Then have the youngster cut the cabbage at the stem, leaving several big leaves on the plant (more baby cabbages will come for later harvest).
- **Bell peppers.** Little gardeners get impatient with bell peppers and want to pick them when they're small. But explain that if the pepper is allowed to ripen to full size (and turn the appropriate color if you've planted a colored variety), they will taste much sweeter. When it comes time to harvest, have the junior SFGer cut the bell pepper off the plant using the handy dandy SFG scissors.
- **Flowers.** Flowers with long or short stems can be cut for indoor display in big or little vases. No matter what, though, it's wise to cut off faded or dead flowers to keep the SFG box looking its best.

For any of the root crops, your child can use their finger and gently dig around the stem where it goes into the ground to get a peek of how big it is. Tell your child to pull the biggest one first and let the rest grow larger for the next harvest.

But Wait, There's More...

Just because the young Square Foot Gardener has harvested everything there was to take out of a given square in their Square Foot Garden, it doesn't mean that the growing has come to a close. In Square Foot Gardening, we take advantage of both hot- and cool-weather crops, to keep our gardens going as long as possible.

We explain to young Square Foot Gardeners that they don't need to settle for just one harvest. Why? Because plants grow in seasons. Does everybody know what seasons are? I like to have Preschool Growers and Early Learners make a chart or big piece of art describing what they think seasons mean. You'd be surprised at all the creative things they can come up with. Use the exercise to focus on the change in temperature between seasons. "Is it cooler in summer or in fall? How about spring and fall?"

Terrific Tweens and Cultivating Teens can do more of a chart (although they can include art elements if they want) explaining what they know about the seasons. What are the key differences between seasons? Are seasons the same across the country?

Have your child make a chart of the seasons and talk with her about how the changing seasons affect a garden.

Succession planting basically comes down to "out with the old, in with the new." Discuss the idea with your gardener. When the radishes are all done, what should you do? Let the ground sit idle, or plant a fall crop, like spinach.

Fall flowers are among the most beautiful. If your youngster is interested in growing some pretty flowers, try to plan it so you will have flowers that bloom in spring, summer, and fall. Cornflowers are a great choice for fall flowers.

This is a good way to start off a discussion that different plants prefer to grow at different times during the year. Those differences mean we can plant one crop right after another. For instance, radishes (a spring, cool-weather root crop) can be followed with bush beans (a summer, warm-weather fruit crop), which can be followed by spinach (a fall, cool-weather leaf crop). There are more, so let's get the young gardeners doing some research—going back and checking their seed catalogs, doing searches online, and visiting nurseries to see what transplants are being offered for the next season.

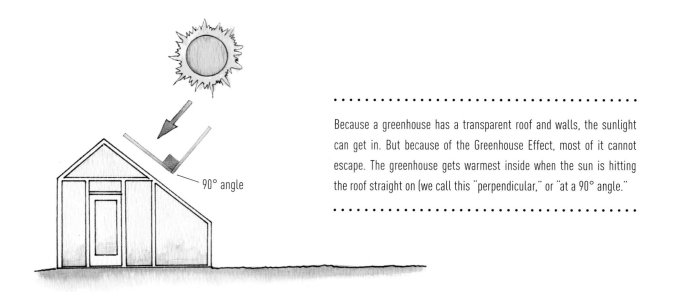

 90° angle

Because a greenhouse has a transparent roof and walls, the sunlight can get in. But because of the Greenhouse Effect, most of it cannot escape. The greenhouse gets warmest inside when the sun is hitting the roof straight on (we call this "perpendicular," or "at a 90° angle."

Extend the Harvest

It's wonderful to get two or three harvests from each of the squares in a child's Square Foot Garden, but what if children could actually extend the growing period right into winter, and maybe beyond? A year-round SFG? Wow, I bet that's something that could really get the kids excited. Ask your youngster: Can they figure out a way to do that?

Most will come up with the idea of moving their Square Foot Garden box indoors. Well, let's think through that option. Is there room in the house or garage for your SFG box? Okay. How much sunlight will the box get indoors? Are Mom and Dad going to be happy with a box right in the middle of their house?

I'm betting "no" is the answer to that one. So maybe there is another option. If we can't put the SFG in the house, maybe we can put a house on the SFG!

The Greenhouse Idea

A greenhouse is a great way to teach groups of kids about gardening and science. The discussion might go like this: Let's get kids to put up a show of hands from everybody who has ever been in a greenhouse. Great. Now, can anybody tell us what a greenhouse is? Alright, let's come up with an explanation. Is it like a regular house? Not really. A greenhouse is transparent. The walls are either made of glass or plastic. The sun shines into the greenhouse. The sun-warmed air is trapped inside by the glass or plastic, so it stays warm for a long time inside the greenhouse, even on cold days. As long as the sun is shining, the greenhouse will be warmer than the temperature outside.

Science Discovery

Scientists that study the environment and Earth's climate are called *climatologists*. Let's see if we have any climatologists among our junior Square Foot Gardeners. Ask your child if he or she has ever heard of the "greenhouse effect." The greenhouse effect is when the Earth's atmosphere does the same thing a greenhouse does—traps the sunlight and warms the air. When the effect is made stronger by more carbon dioxide in the air, the Earth can get warmer and warmer. Let's ask all our **Terrific Tweens** and **Cultivating Teens** to play climatologist and research the answers to some basic questions about the greenhouse effect.

1. What role does pollution, like car exhaust, play in the greenhouse effect?

2. How does the ocean influence the greenhouse effect? How about trees and forests? How about your own Square Foot Garden compared to big backyard single-row gardens in terms of best land use, water use, and amount grown in a given space?

3. Do buildings have anything to do with the greenhouse effect? What about cities? What about farms and ranches?

4. What happens to the weather and the seasons with the greenhouse effect?

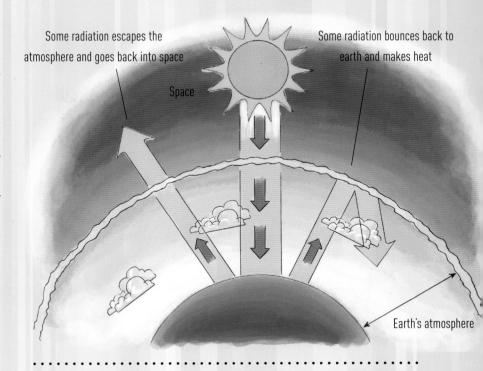

Some radiation escapes the atmosphere and goes back into space

Space

Some radiation bounces back to earth and makes heat

Earth's atmosphere

The Greenhouse Effect is a scientific principle that explains why the sunlight will come into our atmosphere and warm things up, but can't escape back into space. It is the same reason greenhouses keep plants warm inside.

Let's have kids create a big drawing or painting of their findings. The poster should describe how the greenhouse effect works, and what the signs of the effect are.

We don't want to build a whole new greenhouse, do we? We don't really need to, because we already have our SFG boxes; all we have to do is find a way to cover them with a transparent material so that they work like a greenhouse. There are couple ways to do that. One is to create a type of window and frame that go over top of the SFG box. We call this, a "cold frame."

The other and much simpler and inexpensive way to do it is to create a tall, lightweight frame that supports plastic sheeting draped over the box. We call this a "dome." This is pretty easy and something that we do all the time for Square Foot Gardens. Sure sounds like a fun building project for young Square Foot Gardeners, doesn't it?

It's incredible how many neat projects kids can choose from once they get familiar with Square Foot Gardening. Here's another one: a dome cover that can protect the plants in a child's SFG box and can also serve as a makeshift greenhouse to keep plants growing right into (and maybe through) winter.

First, though, we should explore what a dome is, so that we can fit a little geometry into our building lessons. We need to answer the question, what is a dome? Even younger children may have an idea of what a dome is, and older children can research the actual definition. But for our purposes, a dome is a rounded structure we put on top of the SFG box. It is higher than it is wide and starts with the square bottom of the box. It will protect the box from what we call "nibblers," animals like deer. It also keeps any hungry insects away from the box.

But here's the thing: if we cover the dome with thick white or clear plastic, we make a type of greenhouse. The

Converting your SFG box into a genuine greenhouse is easy and fun.

sunlight warms the air inside the dome and it's trapped, keeping your plants nice and toasty even when it's cold outside. And you know what's even better? Any snow, rain, or sleet just slides down the side of the dome, so it won't put too much weight on the structure, and keeps the soil and plants inside safe from the elements. Once plants have established and the weather has warmed, you should put the dome away until next spring.

Tell your child that making a dome for the box isn't a big project. We are just going to build a simple frame and then cover it with plastic. That sounds pretty easy, doesn't it? Okay then, let's get started.

BUILD YOUR OWN:
Dome Greenhouse

We need to do another shopping trip with mom or dad. Kids should bring along the SFG Journal so that they can make notes of what they spend and what they buy.

1. Once at the home center, head to the plumbing department. Ask an associate there for ½-inch PVC pipe, then tell them you would like two 10-foot lengths. You'll also need to buy a small package of plastic cable ties (you can find them in the electrical department) and a heavy plastic drop cloth measuring at least 12 foot by 12 foot (this is called 6-mil polyethylene sheeting). Now you'll need to pick up four 18-inch long, ½-inch (no. 4) pieces of rebar and four 9-inch long pieces of PVC tubing, but if you can't find them that's OK—they're mostly optional. Don't forget to let your child help load and unload the car: it's a great habit to get them into.

2. Here's the best way to anchor your dome: hammer a piece of rebar into each of the inside corners of the SFG box. Then, slip one piece of ¾-inch PVC over each piece of rebar. Slip one end of one of the ½-inch PVC pipes inside the ¾-inch PVC. If the child has any trouble doing this, they should enlist the help of an adult. Here's the easiest ay to anchor your dome: with the box full of Mel's Mix, poke the end of one piece of tubing into the mix and press it all the way down to the bottom of the box. Then, bend it across to the opposite corner and set the other end into the mix the same way. The ½" PVC tubing bends well and doesn't kink or break. If you are using rebar and tubes, bend the PVC pipe over and secure the opposite end of the pipe onto the rebar in the diagonal corner.

Continued on next page

Continued from previous page

. . . .

3. Make a second arch crossing the first, with the ends secured in each corner in the same way. If you did not anchor the tubes onto rebar, it's probably smart to drill a pilot hole into the end of each tube and drive a deck screw to help keep things from blowing away.

. . . .

4. Secure the point at which the arches cross with a nylon cable tie. Sometimes little hands have a hard time working with plastic ties, so you may need to ask Mom or Dad, or your older brother or sister for help doing this.

. . . .

5. Cut a piece of sheet plastic that's big enough to cover the whole dome, with a couple of feet extra on each edge of the box.

6. Drape the plastic over the arch, so there is an equal amount on all sides. You'll need to fold over the sheeting at the corners. Put bricks or stones on the edges of the sheeting to make sure it doesn't blow away in the wind. Congratulations, you've made your own dome greenhouse.

Living History

Terrific Tweens and **Cultivating Teens** can work with the idea of an SFG dome to really dive down and learn something more about architecture and history. That's because the dome on your Square Foot Garden isn't a new invention. I wish I could take credit for the shape, but domes date back thousands of years. Why not have your older gardeners go to the library or go online to discover a bit more about this fascinating shape. Here are some questions they can consider:

1. What are some of the most famous domed buildings?

2. What do you think are the most beautiful domes in history?

3. What is unique about a dome's architecture?

4. Name some countries and civilizations that used domes in their buildings.

5. What is a "geodesic" dome and how does it differ from other domes?

The geodesic dome is a famous architectural form that was created to be strong and simple. What does it have in common with your SFG box dome? How are they different?

Once again, SFG becomes a launch pad for a whole new line of inquiry. Can you imagine what else kids might learn from a simple, little garden bed in the backyard?

Your veggies won't look like this in winter if you've protected them with your SFG dome. But some vegetables, especially those in the cole family, can withstand cold and even snow and taste all the better for it when you pick them.

Square Foot Gardening in Winter

Fresh-picked salad in the middle of winter? I love to tell kids they can get that from their garden because it amazes them. Their eyes get big as saucers. But it's true. With the help of your SFG dome and a few other tricks, your child can be picking fresh lettuce in December, even in some of the coldest climates.

Tell your little Square Foot Gardener that we need to ensure the soil in their SFG box stays warm and never freezes. So in addition to putting on the sheet plastic dome, and making sure that there are no big openings for cold air to get in, the child needs to bank soil up against the outsides of the box (or they can use bales of straw).

The next step is to buy the right seeds. Work with your child to find fast-growing, cold-resistant varieties. A lot of times the name of the variety will be a giveaway. For instance, "Frosty" carrots are meant to be grown in cold seasons.

Even with the dome on top, the box will need all the sun it can get. So plan on moving it, if there is a sunnier spot in the colder months. You want the box to get as much sun as possible. Remember, the sun is in a much different place, and lower in the sky. So take that into account.

The Off Season

If your child isn't growing under cover in the winter, they'll need to "put their SFG to bed." I always tell kids that shutting down a Square Foot Garden over the winter is a lot like when they go to bed. They know that they have to brush their teeth, wash their face and hands, and put on their pajamas before they go to bed. It would be pretty silly to slide into bed with your clothes and shoes still on, right? So the Square Foot Garden needs to be "put to bed" too. It doesn't take much work, but it will set the Square Foot Garden up for a great start next season.

The first thing to do is to point out to kids what needs to be tidied up. All dead foliage and plant debris should be removed from the SFG box. Where the Mel's Mix is low in any given square, let's have the child add a trowelful of compost. Have your child level off the top of the soil and make sure that the watering pail, trowel, and scissors are all cleaned, dried, and brought into the garage or shed.

It is best to clean and fold up your grid to store in the garage for the winter. Cold and wet weather will ruin both wood and plastic. That was certainly easy, wasn't it?

Let's not forget to have kids write down any last impressions in their SFG Journal. Ask your child:

- What was your favorite part about Square Foot Gardening?
- What were your favorite vegetables?
- Which ones would you like to change next season?
- Was the box in the right location?
- Should we put it somewhere else next year?
- Do you think we should do more than one box next season?"

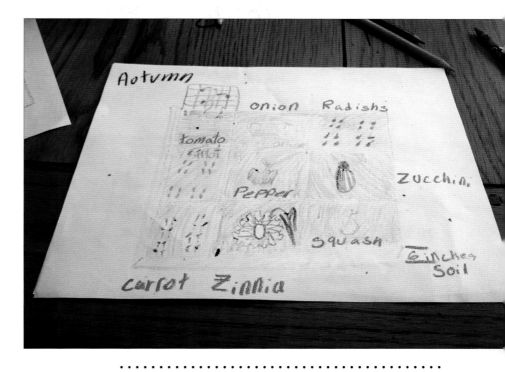

Encourage your young gardeners to make drawings and sketches about this year's garden, and to continue planning for next year. It's one of the best parts of gardening: planning and dreaming for the coming year during the cold of winter.

Preschool Growers and some Early Learners will fill their journal with sketches, clipped out art, or other visuals to help them remember what worked in their Square Foot Garden and what they might want to change. Terrific Tweens and Cultivating Teens can look to make more detailed notes, lists of plants they prefer and those they want to substitute, things they might do differently, and any other ideas or observations they have. It's a wonderful exercise in writing, and gives kids the opportunity to express themselves and learn to write for the pure pleasure of writing.

FUN WITH ART:
The Holiday Box

Just because your child isn't actively growing anything in the box doesn't mean they can't interact with it. Why don't we take the opportunity of the off-season lull in the Square Foot Garden to get children's creative juices flowing, with what we call The Holiday Box.

I've always found that having children decorate their SFG box for different holidays gives them an even greater connection to their SFG, and keeps them anticipating the new growing season. (Some children even like to keep an "SFG calendar" on which they mark off the days till they can plant their box for the new season. That's a nice tradition, don't you think?) Another good idea for winter activities is treats for the birds right at your SFG box. If you have a vertical frame, you can leave the Christmas decorative pine tree branches woven in and out of the netting (remember, the netting won't rot or break) and start hanging pinecones filled with peanut butter for the birds and maybe squirrels. Boy, will that be fun to watch. And don't forget to take a lot of pictures and share them with friends and family.

Try decorating your Square Foot Gardening box for the off-season holidays, like Halloween.

More Seasonal Decorating Fun

There's just no reason at all to allow your SFG boxes to be boring in the off-season. You can start at the Thanksgiving holiday by staking dried stalks of corn (so they don't fall over) for a nice fall look. Put some oversized pumpkins in as well. Find a few boldly colored sheets or large tablecloths at a yard sale or dollar store, and you've got some great SFG box decorations. Put your chicken-wire cover in place and wrap it with a sheet in the color that suits the holiday—Thanksgiving, Christmas, or even New Year's—and secure the sheet in place down along the sides with a bungee cord. That will hold the sheet tightly in place and make it look really nice.

You can even put Christmas lights on your vertical SFG support, but please don't use the blinking kind; people would call that a blinking Square Foot Garden and we tend not to like that.

There's so much kids can do to celebrate the holidays with the SFG box. With the help of Mom and Dad, they can run an extension cord to the box and have eerie lights in a pumpkin for Halloween (along with miniature gravestones for each square!), and multicolored lights for Christmas. They can make signs, sculptures, wreaths, and just about any decoration they want, for every holiday. This gives kids a great way to celebrate and enjoy holidays, and can be fun for the whole family— and just imagine how proud your son or daughter will be when friends or family drop by and see that beautifully decorated Square Foot Gardening box! Why, they might even want an SFG for their house.

By now, your child has discovered and explored the wonderful world of Square Foot Gardening. They've learned lots and lots of lessons, and had hours of fun. But all that doesn't have to stop at the boundaries of your backyard. Children can learn even more valuable lessons by taking what they know about SFG out into the larger world, and helping others enjoy the benefits and pleasures of Square Foot Gardening.

ARE YOU
SQUARE?
quarefootgarden

6

Digging Deeper:
Reaching Out Beyond the Box

It should come as no surprise that I, the Man in the Hat, have been a big promoter of SFG as a way to address many local and global issues. I've seen how an SFG community garden can transform a neighborhood into a thriving social center. I've also been around the world and helped the poor and underprivileged become more independent and realize better lives through growing their own Square Foot Gardens. There is a place on the world stage for SFG, a big role that this novel system can play in ending world hunger and helping all of us eat and live better. That's why if SFG is going to have the sort of impact I know it can, it will be because of Square Foot Gardeners who go out in the world and carry the message directly to the people it can help.

There's a big opportunity in that—the chance to teach kids valuable and lasting lessons about citizenship, charitable works, community and what strong communities are all about, and much more. Those aren't the kind of lessons that translate to good test scores in class, but they can be every bit as valuable. And they sure look good on the child's resume for college, and later, for a job.

Square Foot Gardening has gone global. Through the outreach work of the Square Foot Gardening Foundation we have travelled to dozens of countries to spread the word and teach the benefits of this method that can be used to grow food in even the most unhospitable climates.

SFG in the Schools: A Teacher's Story

Hi, my name is Sandy and I am a 4th grade teacher. I've found Square Foot Gardening to be the perfect vehicle for learning. Though I teach in the California public school system, I find my students learn best when I'm learning about something that interests me, right alongside of them. That is how SFG came to be the center of my classroom. Growing my own vegetables appeals to me on many levels. I love to eat fresh food, am interested in being healthy, and like to share what I cook with the people I love.

Gardening has always been on the list of things I wanted to add to my life. But I had never attempted to grow anything more than a houseplant, and truthfully, not very successfully. I strongly believe that I can learn and be successful at whatever I choose, and decided it was time to give gardening a serious try. I searched the Internet for the most efficient and successful gardening method I could find. I wanted to start with a small garden that would be easy and manageable. As I researched, Mel Bartholomew's Square Foot Gardening method stood out. It met all my requirements and stirred enough optimism in my ability to succeed that I ordered his book. As I began to read, I was inspired to give it a try and was as sure as he was that I'd succeed.

I find the things that inspire me will inspire my students. So I brought my interest and enthusiasm for Mel's book into the classroom and shared what I was doing with my students. I asked them if they would be interested in doing the same. They matched my curiosity and optimism step for step. I sat them down in front of me, opened the book, and began to read. As I read, we chatted about what we might be able to do at our school. Mel's voice came through clearly, enough so that my students wanted to write him a letter. So we wrote him a letter.

The students each contributed a question or comment that we composed together into one email, and we sent him our thoughts. We were very excited when Mel responded. He not only responded, he wrote back speaking to each student about the comment or question each child had written. That was very powerful.

I work hard to teach the students that no matter who the expert or hero, those same experts were all once children sitting in a classroom just as they are now, people who followed their own interests and curiosities. In this case, Mel was the author of a book on a subject he felt passionate about, and we were studying it to build a successful garden. This opens up endless possibilities in these little learners about becoming the author that learns about and shares, in some way, the information on whatever topic sparks their interest.

The math, reading, writing, science, and social study lessons evolved naturally as we made our way through researching, building, and growing our SFG. There is something delightful that happens when a math, reading, writing, science, or social study skill is learned in the midst of discovery, rather than from a workbook. In our pursuit of a successful school garden, the students and I found an abundance of opportunities that stirred curiosity, a need to find answers, or a desire to experiment with just how a certain aspect of the SFG would work for us. I had specific standards to teach according to district and state guidelines. I used what the students did with their SFG to teach and apply those skills, which facilitated their learning. I remember feeling excited as the teacher and watching my students get excited about what we'd be doing next with our garden as the school days progressed. That feeling is something neither my students nor I feel when we work on skills out of a workbook. If you're a teacher, in any capacity, I invite you to take SFG into the classroom. You and your students will be truly amazed at the results.

More and more teachers are turning to Square Foot Gardening as a hands-on exercise to illustrate many lessons in many subject areas.

Starting Local: The Child's First Community Garden

Joining a community garden can be a wonderful experience for a child. The trick is in finding one that will allow both children and a Square Foot Garden. Existing community gardens often have a waiting list. Some community gardens may not allow youngsters to garden alone. A good place to start is online. Your son or daughter will easily be able to find local, state and national community garden associations (see Resources, page 185) with a general web search. Another place to look is your local County Extension Office. Don't know what the Extension System is? Time for a history lesson.

Living History

The Cooperative Extension System is a special branch of the United States Department of Agriculture, created to help farmers and others grow food as efficiently as possible. It's called "Extension" because the organization "reaches out" (like extending your arm) to help communities with their agricultural needs. The roots of the service were planted way back in 1862, when the government passed a law called The Morrill Act. That act created land-grant universities, giving colleges land for free if they would include agricultural programs in what they taught. Then, the Extension System was founded in 1914 (can you count how many years ago that was?). The system has been operating ever since, helping local farmers and gardeners find the best varieties to grow, identify and eradicate pests and diseases, and giving advice on local growing conditions. There are currently 2,900 Extension Offices throughout the country, one in almost every county.

How about we give **Terrific Tweens** and **Cultivating Teens** some questions for further research?

- Who was president when the Extension System was founded?

- What act of congress created the Extension System?

- What wartime garden program did the Extension System help develop?

Unfortunately, today the Extension System does not teach or embrace the Square Foot Gardening method. You can help change that by sending a letter or email to your local Extension Office, asking them to start a program teaching Square Foot Gardening. It's one more way we can help people grow their own food and eat better and healthier.

Finding a Community Garden

If you and your kids are searching for a place to start a community garden, begin by contacting your local parks and recreation department. Check out their websites, because these departments often provide listings of community gardens. Of course, you and your child might just pass by a community garden that looks inviting. Many of these put up a sign with a telephone number for more information. If the garden is open, why not go right inside and ask some questions (or have your youngster take the initiative)? Do they allow children gardeners? Are they aware of Square Foot Gardening and would they be open to having a corner of the garden converted into an SFG box or two? Sometimes the process of dealing with the powers that be in a local community garden involves educating them about Square Foot Gardening. It's a great way for your child to realize how much they have learned about SFG and how even children have the power to teach!

Many cities and larger towns have actively growing community garden resources. They provide an opportunity to get access to garden land, usually with good sunlight. They also provide an opportunity to meet other interested gardeners in your community. If you set up an SFG in a community garden, be prepared to answer some questions.

Preventing vandalism in a community garden

I've found that vandalism isn't as much a problem as you might think, but I know people can get discouraged when it happens in a community garden. Nobody wants to show up to their garden only to find plants dug up or stomped down and the garden a mess. Start by making sure everyone in the neighborhood knows what the garden is about. Put up large sign announcing that it is a community garden serving the neighborhood. Of course, fences make good neighbors in any case, and no more so than with a community garden where they will keep out stray dogs as well as potential vandals.

On the same note, you can plant thorny plants along the edges of the garden, although I think this usually detracts from the garden and doesn't provide enough of a barrier to individuals set on damaging the garden.

Lastly, you can alert the neighborhood watch or residents whose homes overlook the garden to keep their eyes peeled for any problems in the garden. It's always a good idea to get as many people as possible involved in a community garden, even if they aren't doing the gardening themselves!

If you do find space in a local community garden, children may find that they are Square Foot Gardening pioneers. At first, other gardeners may question what the youngster is doing when he first sets up his box. That's a chance for them to develop patience, tolerance, and confidence. Because as odd as the SFG box, Mel's Mix, and the grid may seem to row gardeners in the community garden, just wait. Come early summer when the rest of the garden is being overwhelmed by weeds and unpicked excess produce, the Square Foot Garden box will be neat and tidy as ever, growing wonderfully delicious and easy-to-harvest crops. The advantage will be clear for everyone to see and then the questions will change. How do I build one of those boxes? What is that grid about? How come you never need to weed? Why do you keep a pail of water by your box? It usually only takes one season to convert the rest of the community garden. And then won't your youngster be proud of working through the negative comments and barrage of questions?

SFG ACTIVITY:
Start a Community Garden

Teens with a lot of energy and the need for a good high school project can consider starting their own community garden. Although it takes a lot of energy, time, and dedication, it can be an unforgettable experience and an unparalleled resume builder for college. To start with, the teen should enlist as much help as possible, including friends and other Square Foot Gardeners, Mom and Dad, other family members, and key stakeholders in the community (such as local government officials and teachers).

1. The first step is to find appropriate land. It's going to be either public or private. Public land might be school grounds, parkland, or recreational centers. Private land could be a churchyard, open lots, or private and vacant lots. It could even be a parking lot at a commercial location. No matter where the location, the lot will need a water supply and some sort of protection around it. It will also need full sunlight. And that's about it. Doesn't matter if it's paved; we'll build our boxes and sit them right on the pavement. Doesn't matter if there's bad soil, or if a building used to be there. We're going to lay down our weed fabric and put bottoms on our boxes as necessary. Kids can even elevate the boxes with a couple bricks or cinderblocks.

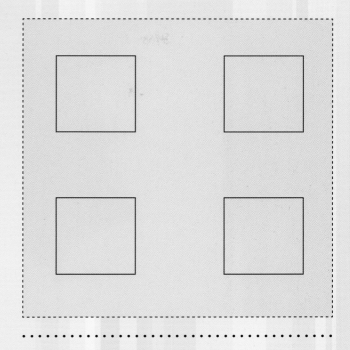

These are standard measurements for the SFG boxes in one corner of a community garden. The measurements are optimal, but can be altered slightly to suit the particular circumstances of your community garden. Keep in mind that the boxes may be reshaped to accommodate an oddly shaped lot. For instance, rather than 4 × 4 feet, a box might be 2 × 8 feet, or two 4 × 4-foot boxes can be turned into a 4 × 8-foot box.

Continued on next page

Continued from previous page

2. The next thing is to find the owner and approach with all the pros and cons ready, in writing. It's worth mentioning to the owner or owners that they would get some good publicity and newspaper coverage if they let kids start a children's community garden on their land. But here's my advice from real experience: Make it small. Do a trial the first year. Teens will have to discuss with the owner what they can and can't do. The owner of the land will want certain rules and regulations. These conditions go into the formal rules and regulations. Teens will need their parents' help to list in writing the important conditions about the land. How long will this lease last? And how can it be renewed? You don't want to put a lot of time, effort, and money into something and find out that the owners decided to sell the land after a year, and you have to leave and move everything.

3. Work out space allocation. Each person that signs up gets room for so many boxes. Teens will also have to figure out how much to charge. They should check around and see what the going rate is for community gardens. Sometimes it's as low as $5 per year, sometimes as high as $25 a year. The money will go toward water and administrative services, and should probably be handled by parents or teachers.

4. Lay out the garden, accommodating the particular size and location. They'll want a fairly wide central path, right down through the middle (assuming it's a rectangular shape, like the size of a house lot). That center aisle should be at least 4, if not 5, feet wide. Branching off that should be sub-paths 3 feet wide. Kids can almost think of this as a street of houses, but instead of house there are going to be garden plots. They can drive stakes and use twine to mark off 10-foot x 10-foot plots. Each plot will have a front entrance, and two or three garden plots next to them.

Remember to keep it small to start with. The kids can always expand later. Everyone dreams big, but the truth is, people often get overwhelmed with too much to do, too much to take care of. So even if the kids have managed to secure a large lot for the garden, they don't necessarily have to fill it with boxes and spaces the first year.

SFG Activity

Whether teens are considering a community garden or just joining together to create a group garden in a large backyard, here's a wonderful way for them to record shade and shadows in the space. Have them take a digital picture of the lot every one to two hours throughout the day, standing in the same spot. If they already own a digital camera, that would be great, or you can lend them yours. Of course, most cell phones these days have their own cameras built in and those cameras will work just as well (and might be a lot handier).

Looking for a place to start a garden, community based or otherwise? The great thing about Square Foot Gardening is that you can start a garden even in a vacant spot with no soil.

The photos don't need to be professional quality. Now the images can be made into an electronic "slideshow" that represents the movement of shadows throughout the day. That's a neat way for kids to get a clear idea of how shade will affect the site of their future community garden, and the process helps them develop photographic (and presentation) skills along the way!

Groups and SFG

The more Square Foot Gardening children do, the more confident they become in the method. That makes them ideal SFG ambassadors. The kids are sure to ask, "What's an ambassador?" Of course, an ambassador is a representative, someone who promotes a cause or interest to other people. So we let children know that if they enjoyed all the fun they had with Square Foot Gardening, they can become SFG ambassadors. But how can a child be an ambassador? The best way to start is with any group that the child is already a member of.

Scouts. Imagine how fun Square Foot Gardening would be for a whole troop of Boy Scouts or Girl Scouts. If your child is a member of a scout troop, they can earn a merit badge or insignia in gardening or the environment with their very first SFG. But they can also get the whole troop involved in a community garden, or in growing gardens to help the elderly. Kids might be able to earn a slew of badges by the time they harvest their Square Foot Gardens! Applying for the badge or insignia will require initiative, and working with other scouts to form a larger garden will require teamwork, leadership, and cooperation. Those are all as important as any school lessons children may learn from the SFG.

Clubs. What about clubs like the 4-H club? Those would be a natural place to get people involved in SFG, wouldn't it? There are 4-H clubs all around the country, and they can be an excellent way for children to meet other kids interested in agriculture, as well to get the word out about SFG. But even if there isn't a club in your vicinity, or if you child doesn't want to join, clubs can still be a good way to fire up interest in SFG.

School. Because there are so many lessons you can learn from Square Foot Gardening, schools are natural places for SFG. Have your children ask their teacher about starting one or more SFGs in the schoolyard as a special project. This is a chance for youngsters to show off all they've learned about SFG, and demonstrate all the learning potential inside an SFG box. A school class can start with one box and then expand the garden so that all the children get their own boxes. Teachers can even find a lesson plan on the Square Foot Gardening Foundation website (see Resources, page 185).

SFG Activity

Kids don't necessarily need to join a community garden to start a community of Square Foot Gardeners. Do you have a little extra space in your backyard? Why not help your children start a backyard gardening club? It's a great way to get kids busy (especially over the long summer break) and have them nearby so that parents can keep an eye on everyone. Once your child understands the basics, they can pass on their knowledge to other neighborhood kids who can grow their own SFGs in their own yards. The kids can decide on a club name, make a club flag, and even have a secret club handshake! It's a great way for kids to work through the decisions, like choosing plants—everyone can discover what they need to know together. They can also share what works best for them, and help each other get the best harvest possible. You can sponsor contests for the longest carrot or biggest beet. Even better, the best photograph of a garden. You could even make up medals for the best gardeners—or have the kids design their own!

What could be more fun that a community garden of Square Foot Gardens? So many opportunities to learn and teach.

SFG as Volunteer Activity

Kids can use what they've learned about Square Foot Gardening as a way to give back to the community, reinforce religious or spiritual beliefs, and build a resume for college or job applications. That's because there are many people who can benefit from SFG but can't do it all themselves. Close to home, youngsters can do good by introducing elderly grandparents to SFG. If the grandparents are unable to garden because of mobility, strength, or other issues, an older child can set up an SFG box near a window. That way, grandparents can enjoy the garden even if they can't work in it. With a child's help, the grandparents can even eat a salad a day—all organic and healthy. What better gift for the grandparents?

Kids can also use their SFG skills to help out in their communities. One of the terrific things about a Square Foot Garden is that it can be portable. All a child has to do is put a bottom on the box, and they can create a garden for patients in a hospital (put the box on a gurney to let the patient work on the garden bedside, and then roll it out in the parking lot to get sun!), or for the residents of a nursing home. Just imagine all the smiles when a child wheels in a garden box filled with delicious vegetables and pretty flowers, for elderly people who can't get out to a garden themselves. If a regular size child's box is a little too big for your child to handle when it's portable, they can always make smaller boxes. Maybe they want to make 1 x 1 boxes for people at the nursing home. Everyone gets a different square and a different plant. Wouldn't that be wonderful?

Reaching Out

One of the best gifts Square Foot Gardening can give kids is a wider worldview. Use the garden to start a discussion about how we grow food in the world, and why so many people around the globe go to bed hungry.

This can be an important social studies investigation. We know that hundreds of millions of people don't get enough to eat in any given day. That's amazing isn't it? Wouldn't it be great to solve that problem? Why not get kids involved in thinking about that and doing some research to get to the roots of the problem.

Is the real problem that there is not enough food, or is there another cause? Where is world hunger the biggest problem? What other problems does hunger cause? How is world hunger tied to climate change? What other things affect world hunger? Can we think of some solutions? How can SFG help?

Kids should take this chance to learn about other cultures, like India, Central America, or the nations of Africa. It's also a good way to teach even small children about world geography.

St. John's Baptist Church in Columbia, South Carolina, has a food pantry that hands out hundreds of pounds of food every week, in partnership with a local food bank, Columbia Harvest Hope. St. John's had a community garden—a row garden full of weeds and very neglected. At the same time, Columbia College had been working on a community project to fight Type II diabetes. Their program involved a model for health awareness, including a walking program, a crockpot cooking program, and a gardening element. The idea was that these three components would serve to teach people about their disease and to be proactive in managing it—as well as any health problem—rather than turning only to prescription drugs. St. John's, Columbia College, and the Square Foot Gardening Foundation joined forces to realize the third (gardening) leg of the program with a 10-box SFG created in one weekend in an empty lot on church property. The garden is flourishing with organic fruits, vegetables, herbs, and flowers. It's a great example of how different elements within the community—in this case, a church, a college, and a non-profit—can come together and create a valuable asset in a community garden.

Science Discovery

Mapping world hunger can be a revealing and character-building exercise, especially for older kids. To start with, we'll need a big, blank world map. You can find these online and you may be able to locate them in a local store, but I like the idea of kids making their own maps as a big art project. It gives them the chance to become familiar with world geography.

Use a world atlas or have your kids print out a world map from an online source. Then they can copy the shape of the continents on a big piece of posterboard or a large piece of paper. (Butcher paper can be excellent for this, or the kids may find their own large canvas for making a world map.)

Now the children can research each country, continent, or area in turn. They can start to fill in the country borders as they learn where everything is located. Lastly, they should go to the library or do research online to start filling in the map with markings for where hunger is a problem. They can use color or graphics like lines or symbols. Either way, the idea is to see where world hunger is clustered and learn more about its causes and effects.

They can write to the President, their congressional representatives, or even state officials (kids can easily find all those addresses online). But they can also write or email the World Food Programme, a non-profit, non-governmental organization that supplies food to those in need around the globe. There are several other non-profit organizations that work to solve world hunger, and those can be found in listings in the library, or through Internet searches.

Once children know who they want to send the letter to, they still need to figure out what it is they should say in the letter. Some kids will need help writing their letters, and teachers or parents can urge them to keep it simple. What is the point of the letter? If you're promoting SFG as a solution to hunger, you'll need to say why it would be a good solution (things like, "doesn't take much money, saves 90 percent of the water, easy to do anywhere, don't need a lot of knowledge or equipment"). That's all good. What else? Oh yeah, how much it provides per box. A salad a day! That can certainly go a long way to heading off hunger, can't it?

In my experience, kids really feel involved when they write letters to authorities. The more children that write, the more the authorities take notice. Imagine if we can get governments and organizations around the globe promoting the use of Square Foot Gardening for the poor and hungry of the world! If SFG helps eradicate world hunger, your child can truly say that they played a part in that. Wouldn't that be something incredible to carry through life?

Taking Action

I've traveled around the world to help local communities start their own SFGs to become more independent and live healthier lives. Those have been very rewarding experiences for me, but obviously, kids aren't going to be able to travel around the globe taking the message of SFG to the underprivileged. So what can they do?

Write letters. This will be a handy lesson in civics and the practice of composing and writing correspondence.

Growing with SFG

It should be clear by now that there is no limit to the things Square Foot Gardening can teach children (and adults, by the way). Inside an SFG box lies lessons in math, science, art, history, vocabulary, and much more. The method also teaches youngsters independence, planning, confidence, and social skills. It's like having a whole school full of teachers and life coaches right there in that 3 x 3 box in your backyard.

Another wonderful thing about SFG is that you never outgrow it. The lessons children learn will stick with them for the rest of their lives, and they can also Square Foot Garden for the rest of their lives. As they do, they'll be eating healthy, doing a favor for the environment, and enjoying nature.

Thank you for reading this book. I hope it inspires your entire family to get involved and use everything I have learned in life to benefit yours and all the others in the world that haven't experienced the joy and benefits of gardening, the Square Foot Gardening way.

7 Kids' Guide to Veggies & Herbs

Every plant you grow in your garden has different needs and requires unique care. Learning to understand your plants and treat them properly is the key to becoming a top-notch gardener. The best way to learn is to study first and then test your knowledge in the field. Each of the following pages has the information you need to know to obtain, plant, grow, and harvest the vegetables and herbs that are best-suited for a kid's Square Foot Garden. There are 26 different plants with profiles. Of course, you can find many more choices than just these 26 at any garden center. To learn more about the rest of the vegetable kingdom, and the flower kingdom too, start by reading the seed packets. Or, go to your library and look up the ones you are interested in in a vegetable book. And there are always the seed catalogs we've talked about throughout this book. They are a fun and handy resource—plus you can get an idea how much some things cost, which is a big help when you're planning your budget in your SFG Journal.

All About Basil

Basil is part of the mint family. 'Sweet Genovese' is a type of basil that's crushed to make into pesto. Basil is used in Italian cooking, as well as many Asian dishes. In India, it is planted around the temples and is a part of some religious ceremonies. Basil also comes in flavors, such as cinnamon, licorice, and lemon. Go ahead and splurge—grow a few different kinds and discover the wonders of this beautiful and delicious herb.

BASIL

BOTANICAL INFORMATION
Family: Mint
Height: 1 to 2 feet
Spacing: small, 4 per square foot large, 1 per square foot
GROWING SEASON
Spring: no
Summer: yes
Fall: no
Winter: no

Seed to Harvest/Flower: 12 weeks
Seeds Storage: 5 years
Weeks to Maturity: 4 to 6 weeks
Indoor Seed Starting: 4 to 6 weeks before last frost
Earliest Outdoor Planting: after soil has warmed
Additional Plantings: 3 weeks and 6 weeks
Last Planting: not needed

One of the most popular basil dishes, along with pesto, is called caprese. It is served cold because it needs no cooking. You simply take a piece of toast (a baguette works great) and give it a light coating of extra virgin olive oil. Then, add a slice of ripe tomato. Top the tomato with a slice of fresh mozzarella cheese (fresh mozzarella comes in a ball shape about the size of a tennis ball). Then, add a nice, big leaf of basil on top. It is a classic flavor combination that most people adore.

Starting

- Location: Full sun.
- Seeds Indoors: Start seeds indoors four to six weeks before the last frost. Seeds germinate quickly.
- Transplanting: Set out after all danger of frost has passed and the soil has warmed. Basil will stop growing if the weather is cool and then take a while to catch up, so wait to transplant basil until the weather is starting to feel like summer.
- Seeds Outdoors: Sow basil seeds where the plants are to be grown in warm soil. Seeds germinate in seven to ten days, and the plants grow quickly.

Growing

- Watering: Keep well-watered.
- Maintenance: Pinch the basil tops often to keep the plant bushy. Harvesting basil for cooking will also keep the plant strong and bushy. For energetic, tasty plants, remove flower buds as they appear.

Harvesting

- How: Pinch stems just above leaf nodes where new stems will sprout. Use only the leaves in cooking.
- When: Harvest basil anytime. In fact, the more you pinch off leaves and stems, the more it will grow.

Preparing and Using

Use fresh leaves in cooking, discarding stems. Dried basil does not retain its flavor. Excess basil can be processed with olive oil, wrapped tightly in plastic wrap, and stored in the freezer for up to three months.

Problems

Aphids and Japanese beetles; Fusarium wilt.

All About Beans

Beans are one of the easiest veggies to grow. They come in two types: bush beans and pole beans. Pole beans like to climb up, so they are great for vertical gardening in your SFG. A lot of gardeners think that pole beans have better flavor, while the bush types taste more like "green beans." Bush beans grow lower to the ground; each plant yields one large crop all at once, with a smaller crop a few weeks later.

Pole beans take longer to grow, but provide a steady continuous yield all season long. A single planting of pole types is adequate, while additional plantings of the bush types are needed to have a constant harvest.

Starting

- Location: Full sun.
- Seeds Indoors: No.
- Transplanting: Does not transplant well.
- Seeds Outdoors: Presoak seeds for 30 minutes for faster sprouting. Plant seeds about an inch deep and water right away. Seeds sprout in five to ten days. For a continuous harvest of bush beans, plant a new square of a different color or variety every two weeks all summer long.

Growing

- Watering: Beans must have regular waterings. Do not allow the soil to dry out, but keep the leaves dry.
- Maintenance: Weed weekly if you see any weeds sprouting.

Harvesting

- How: Picking green beans can be very exciting. They like to hide among the leaves and you can find you're staring right at one without seeing it before it surprises you. Break or cut each stem holding the bean pod. Do not pull on the plant when harvesting.

BEAN

BOTANICAL INFORMATION	
Family: Pulse	
Height:	
Bush: 12 to 18 inches	
Pole: 4 to 7 feet	
Spacing:	
Bush: 9 per square	
Pole: 8 per square	
GROWING SEASON	
Spring: no	
Summer: yes	
Fall: no	
Winter: no	

Seed to Harvest/Flower:
Bush: 8 weeks
Pole: 10 weeks
Seeds Storage: 3 to 4 years
Weeks to Maturity:
Bush: 8 weeks
Pole: 9 weeks
Indoor Seed Starting: no
Earliest Outdoor Planting: immediately after the last spring frost
Additional Plantings: every 2 weeks

- When: Pick beans when they are still small and tender. Do not allow them to get so large that pods bulge with seeds; the plant will stop producing and the best flavor is past.

Preparing and Using

Wash and refrigerate if not using immediately. Beans do not store well, so try to use them the same day they are picked. Beans contain lots of vitamins A, B, and C, as well as calcium and iron.

Beans are good eaten raw when they are small—remember, the smaller the bean, the more tender it will be.

Cook any size bean. They can be steamed, boiled, or stir-fried, then served individually with a little seasoning, grated cheese, or parsley. Beans are excellent additions to soups, stews, or mixed vegetable dishes. Leftovers can be added to a salad; I've even heard of people adding marinated beans to a sandwich, along with lettuce, tomato, and cheese! How does that sound?

Problems

Aphids, Japanese and Mexican bean beetles, birds, rabbits, woodchucks, and deer; blight, rust, and mildew. Sounds like a lot but they are still worthwhile.

All About Beets

Beets are a wonderful vegetable to grow because they're easy and both the roots and the greens (tops) can be eaten. They are mostly pest- and disease-free and resistant to both fall and spring frosts. The root gets very hard when grown in the hot summer season.

BEET

BOTANICAL INFORMATION
  Family: Goosefoot
  Height: 12 inches
  Spacing: 9 or 16 per square
GROWING SEASON
  Spring: yes
  Summer: yes
  Fall: yes
  Winter: no

Seed to Harvest/Flower: 8 weeks
Seeds Storage: 4 to 5 years
Weeks to Maturity: 8 weeks
Earliest Outdoor Planting: 3 weeks before last spring frost
Additional Plantings: every 3 weeks

Starting

- Location: Partial shade or full sun.
- Seeds Indoors: No.
- Transplanting: Does not transplant well.
- Seeds Outdoors: Each seed in the packet is actually a cluster of two to five individual seeds, so several sprouts will come up from each seed planted. Plant one presoaked seed in each space ½ inch deep three weeks **before** the last spring frost. To have a continuous harvest, plant a new square every three weeks except in the hottest part of the summer. After the sprouts are about 1 inch tall, cut off all except the strongest plant from each seed cluster.

Growing

- Watering: Plants need constant and even moisture.
- Maintenance: Keep damaged leaves picked off, mulch in hot weather, and weed weekly.

Harvesting

- How: Pull up the entire plant with the largest top. If you're not sure of bulb size, dig around the root with your fingers to uncover the top to check the size. To harvest greens, individual leaves can be cut at any time, but don't take more than one or two from each plant.
- When: Roots are the most tender when half size, so start pulling when the roots are approximately the size of a Ping-Pong ball and continue until they are full size. Leaves are usable at any size.

Preparing and Using

Use greens whole or chopped in fresh salads, or cook them like spinach. Roots are rich in iron and vitamin B. Serve hot—boiled, steamed or baked with the skin on, then squeeze them to take the skin off (your hands will turn red when you do this). Try sautéing shredded raw beets quickly and serve hot, or try them cooked and chilled (shredded, sliced, or diced) in salads or mixed with cottage cheese. Small whole beets can also be cooked and served with an orange sauce, salad dressing, or a spoonful of sour cream. Try them in a Russian soup called "borsht" that can be served hot or cold.

Problems

Cutworms, slugs and snails, leaf miners, rabbits, woodchucks, and deer. Relatively disease-free.

All About Broccoli

Broccoli requires cool weather but is great in a Square Foot Garden. It is very frost-hardy and grows well in the spring and fall; it doesn't do well in the summer heat. A lot of kids hate broccoli but most adults love it. It's one of those veggies that have an "acquired taste" so even if you haven't liked it before, keep trying it—it will be worth it.

BROCCOLI

BOTANICAL INFORMATION
Family: Mustard
Height: 18 to 24 inches
Spacing: 1 per square

GROWING SEASON
Spring: yes
Summer: no
Fall: yes
Winter: no

Seed to Harvest/Flower: 16 weeks
Seeds Storage: 5 to 6 years
Weeks to Maturity: 9 weeks
Indoor Seed Starting: 12 weeks before last spring frost
Earliest Outdoor Planting: 5 weeks before last spring frost

Starting

- Location: Needs full sun.
- Seeds Indoors: Plant 5 to 10 seeds in a cup of vermiculite, or place one seed ¼ inch deep in potting soil in each individual compartment of a seedling tray, approximately twelve weeks before your last spring frost. Seed will sprout indoors in five to ten days at 70°F. Keep seed warm until sprouted; move to full sunlight as soon as the first shoots appear.
- Transplanting: Plant outside approximately five weeks before the last spring frost.
- Seeds Outdoors: Not satisfactory, as the season is too short before hot weather arrives.

Growing

- Watering: Like all members of the cabbage family (also called the cole family), you're growing leaves and flowers, which need consistent moisture. Never let broccoli dry out or wilt.
- Maintenance: Weed weekly; mulch in warmer weather.

Harvesting

- How: Cut off the main central head at its base with a sharp, serrated knife or clippers, leaving as many leaves on the plant as possible. Within a few weeks, new side-shoots (miniature heads) will form and grow from the original plant to provide you with a second harvest.
- When: Harvest as soon as a head appears full and tight. The head is actually a flower head, which you want to harvest before the flower buds open. If you have several plants, don't wait too long to cut the first one after the heads start forming, even if it looks a little small. It's still edible when it's small.

Preparing and Using

Broccoli contains vitamins A, B, and C, as well as calcium, phosphorus, and iron. Wash under running water and soak in cold salted water for two hours if there's any chance that a green cabbage worm is present in the head. Refrigerate if you're not using immediately. Broccoli can be served fresh and raw with mayonnaise, or any dip, or can be chopped fresh into a salad. To cook it, you can steam, boil, or stir-fry. Try it plain with just a little dressing, sour cream, or topped with a cheese sauce or just plain lemon juice. It's an excellent addition to any stir-fried dish; mix it with interesting combinations of meats and vegetables.

Problems

Cutworms, root maggots, green worms, and cabbage worms; club root.

All About Cabbage

Cabbage is a very easy vegetable to grow. It's frost hardy and takes very little work. Cabbage comes in a variety of shapes, sizes, colors, and leaf textures, and can be grown as an early- to late-season crop; the early-season variety is smaller and faster growing, while the late- or long-season variety is usually bigger. All varieties grow best in cool spring or fall weather.

CABBAGE

BOTANICAL INFORMATION
Family: Mustard
Height: 12 to 18 inches
Spacing: 1 per square
GROWING SEASON
Spring: yes
Summer: no
Fall: yes
Winter: no

Seed to Harvest/Flower: 16 weeks
Seeds Storage: 5 to 6 years
Weeks to Maturity: 9 weeks
Indoor Seed Starting: 12 weeks before last spring frost
Earliest Outdoor Planting: 5 weeks before last spring frost

Starting

- Location: Full sun.
- Seeds Indoors: Plant one seed ¼ inch deep in potting soil in individual compartments of a seedling tray twelve weeks before your last spring frost. Seeds sprout in five to eight days at 70°F. For a second crop in the fall, repeat the process anytime in the middle of June (or back up sixteen weeks from your first fall frost date). In most places you can usually start seeds of a new crop as soon as you've harvested your spring crop. Keep warm (70°F) until sprouted; move to full sunlight as soon as first shoots appear.
- Transplanting: Don't let transplants get too large before planting them outside. Late transplants do not form good heads, and sometimes flower the first year if allowed to get too large.
- Seeds Outdoors: The season is too short to plant seeds directly in the garden for the spring crop, and starting the fall crop from seed outdoors would tie up too much valuable garden space that could be used more productively. Start all seeds in individual containers for transplanting into the garden.

Growing

- Watering: Cabbage needs lots of water to head up properly, but after the head is formed and while it is growing to full size, cut back on watering or the head will grow too fast and split.
- Maintenance: Weed weekly; cut away any extra-large bottom leaves if they are yellow. If large lower leaves are spreading to other squares, cut away any portions that are "over the line." This will not hurt the plant.

Harvesting

- How: Cut off the entire head with a sharp, serrated knife or clippers.
- When: Anytime the head starts to develop and feels firm. If you have several plants, don't wait until all the heads are large. They may split in hot weather and go to seed, and you'll be left with nothing.

Preparing and Using

Cabbage is delicious cooked or raw and contains a lot of vitamin C. You can shred it to make cole slaw, sauerkraut, or a Korean dish called kimchee.

Problems

Slugs and snails, aphids, and cabbage worms (their worst enemy).

All About Carrots

Carrots are related to the wildflower called Queen Anne's lace. The seeds are so small that planting them can be very tedious; practice dropping a pinch (two or three seeds) on some white paper until you get the hang of it. Carrots can be either long and thin or short and stubby; pick the shape and size that best suits your garden. There is nothing more exciting for kids (including kids my age) than pulling up a carrot they planted months ago! It's sort of like fishing—you don't know how big it is until you see it, but you hope it's a whopper.

CARROT

BOTANICAL INFORMATION
  Family: Carrot
  Height: 12 inches
  Spacing: 16 per square
GROWING SEASON
  Spring: yes
  Summer: yes
  Fall: yes
  Winter: yes

Seed to Harvest/Flower: 10 weeks
Seeds Storage: 3 to 4 years
Weeks to Maturity: 10 weeks
Indoor Seed Starting: no
Earliest Outdoor Planting: 3 weeks before last spring frost

Starting

- Location: Full sun, but can stand partial shade.
- Seeds Indoors: No.
- Transplanting: Does not transplant well.
- Seeds Outdoors: Sprouts in two to three weeks outdoors. Seeds are very small; try pelleted seeds if necessary. Plant two or three seeds in each of the 16 spaces in a square. Water soil and cover the square with a plastic-covered cage. Keep the ground moist at all times, even if it means daily spraying in sunny weather.

Growing

- Watering: Carrots must have constant moisture until they're almost mature to grow quickly and continuously. Then reduce watering so the carrots don't crack from overly rapid growth.
- Maintenance: Weed weekly; otherwise carrots are relatively work-free.

Harvesting

- How: Pull up those with the largest tops. If you're not sure which are biggest, dig around the plant with your fingers to test the size.

- When: Pick them early, when they're only half size and at their sweetest and most tender.

Preparing and Using

Scrub with a vegetable brush, but don't peel them. Most of the vitamins are in the skin or close to the surface. Rich in vitamin A and thiamine (vitamin B1), carrots also contain calcium. Carrots are delicious fresh and raw—shredded, sliced thinly, or cut into sticks for snacking. They can be cooked by steaming or boiling. They can be served in a variety of dishes, or added to soups and stews, but seem best when served with a dressing, a dab of sour cream, or sprinkled with parsley and grated cheese. Carrots are so versatile you can even make a wonderfully moist cake with them.

Problems

Carrot rust fly, rabbits, woodchucks, deer, and voles. Virtually disease-free.

All About Swiss Chard

Swiss chard is known best for its vitamin-rich leaves and its succulent stems. It's one of the easiest vegetables to grow in any part of the country, and can be grown in the sun or shade, all spring, summer, and fall for a continuous harvest. Chard is available in white- or red-stemmed varieties and is also available in many rainbow colors. It can have either smooth or crinkled leaves, whichever you like; try both! It is also virtually pest- and disease-free.

Starting

- Location: Does best in full sun, but can grow in partial shade.
- Seeds Indoors: Plant 10 seeds in a cup of vermiculite, or place one seed ½ inch deep in potting soil in individual compartments of a seedling tray seven weeks before your last spring frost. Seeds will sprout in five to ten days at 70°F. Keep warm (70°F) until sprouted; move to full sunlight as soon as first shoots appear.
- Transplanting: Plant into the garden three weeks before the last spring frost.
- Seeds Outdoors: Plant presoaked seeds ½ inch deep in each square three weeks before your last spring frost. Seeds sprout outdoors in two to three weeks.

Growing

- Watering: Weekly, or twice weekly in hot weather. Like all leaf crops, Swiss chard needs lots of water for luxurious leaf growth.
- Maintenance: Weed weekly; cut off any yellow or overgrown outer leaves.

CHARD, SWISS

BOTANICAL INFORMATION
- Family: Goosefoot
- Height: 12 to 18 inches
- Spacing: 4 per square

GROWING SEASON
- Spring: yes
- Summer: yes
- Fall: yes
- Winter: yes

Seed to Harvest/Flower: 8 weeks
Seeds Storage: 4 to 5 years
Weeks to Maturity: 8 weeks
Indoor Seed Starting: 7 weeks before last spring frost
Earliest Outdoor Planting: 3 weeks before last spring frost

Harvesting

- How: Carefully cut off each outer stem at the plant base with a sharp knife when the leaves are 6 to 9 inches tall. The smaller inner leaves will continue to grow.
- When: Start harvesting when the outer leaves are about 6 to 9 inches tall (approximately eight weeks after planting seeds), and continue harvesting outer leaves (stalk and all) every week or so. Don't let outer leaves get too large before harvesting.

Preparing and Using

Both leaves and stems are edible; leaves are very rich in vitamins A and C, calcium, and iron. The stalks can be cooked and served like asparagus; the leaves are used fresh or cooked, and are similar to, but milder in taste than, spinach.

After harvest, rinse and pat dry like lettuce or spinach; refrigerate if not using immediately. Cut out the central stalk and use the leaves as fresh greens for salads, or boil or steam as you would spinach. Add freshly chopped greens to any appropriate soup for a garden-fresh taste.

Problems

Slugs and snails, cutworms, and leaf miners; occasionally rabbits, woodchucks, and deer. Free of most diseases.

All About Chives

This is a fun little plant with a spiky hairdo. Classified as an herb, the slim, round leaves are hollow and have a mild onion scent when cut. The pinkish-purple flowers are edible and appear in late spring and make a pretty garnish for salads. Chives are a member of the onion family, and oddly enough, it is one herb that hasn't really been used for medicinal purposes during its long history. It is simply a unique garden plant that has enhanced the flavor of savory foods for centuries.

CHIVE

BOTANICAL INFORMATION
- **Family:** Lily
- **Height:** 6 to 12 inches
- **Spacing:** 16 per square

GROWING SEASON
- **Spring:** late
- **Summer:** yes
- **Fall:** no
- **Winter:** no

Seed to Harvest/Flower: 16 weeks
Seeds Storage: 2 years
Weeks to Maturity: 10 weeks
Indoor Seed Starting: 10 weeks before last frost
Earliest Outdoor Planting: late spring
Additional Plantings: not needed
Last Planting: not needed

Starting

- Location: Full sun.
- Seeds Indoors: Plant seeds indoors in late winter. Seeds can take up to twenty-one days to germinate.
- Transplanting: Set plants out in spring. Although chives are cold-hardy, it is best to set new plants out after all danger of frost has passed.
- Seeds Outdoors: Sprouts in late spring to early summer.

Growing

- Watering: Keep soil moist.
- Maintenance: Plants will spread, so divide clumps every few years to rejuvenate the plants.

Harvesting

- How: Snip the tips of the leaves as needed to garnish baked potatoes and creamed soups. Don't cut off more than ⅓ of the plant at any one time.
- When: Chives can be harvested anytime after the new leaves have reached 6 to 8 inches. To enjoy the tasty pink flowers, don't harvest the plant until you can see the flower buds, then clip around them or wait until they bloom. The flowers make a lovely garnish.

Preparing and Using

Cut ⅓ of the tops off all leaves if you like the flat-top look, or cut a few leaves down to ⅓ of each leaf. Snip the fresh hollow leaves into salads, sauces, soups, or dips.

Problems

Insufficient water can cause leaf tips to turn brown.

All About Cilantro

The fresh leaf of cilantro is probably the most widely used of all flavoring herbs throughout the world. It is used in Middle Eastern, Indian, Southeast Asian, and South American cuisines. Cilantro is a pretty plant that looks somewhat like parsley. Use it like parsley in smaller quantities for a unique tang. When cilantro goes to seed, it becomes another herb altogether—coriander. Ancients used to chew coriander seeds to combat heartburn (probably after weeding their long single-row gardens). The seeds are sweet when they're ripe, but terribly bitter when immature. Cilantro has a very short growing season, so pick it while it's nice and tender. Once the leaves start to yellow and the plant beings to bolt the taste of leaves is ruined.

Starting

- Location: Full sun to partial shade.
- Seeds Indoors: No.
- Transplanting: Does not transplant well.
- Seeds Outdoors: After last frost.

Growing

- Watering: Weekly.
- Maintenance: Shelter the plants from wind, otherwise cilantro needs little care besides watering.

Harvesting

- How: Pick cilantro leaves as you need them, even if the plant is only 6 inches tall. For coriander seeds, cut whole plants and hang to dry, and then shake the dried seeds into a paper bag.
- When: Harvest the cilantro leaves anytime after the plant has reached 6 to 8 inches. Harvest the seeds (coriander) after the plants have turned brown but before the seeds start to fall. Cilantro self-sows with abandon.

CILANTRO

BOTANICAL INFORMATION
Family: Umbellifer
Height: 1 to 2 feet
Spacing: 1 per square

GROWING SEASON
Spring: late
Summer: yes
Fall: no
Winter: no

Seed to Harvest/Flower: 5 weeks (leaves), 12 weeks (coriander seeds)
Seeds Storage: n/a
Weeks to Maturity: 5 weeks
Indoor Seed Starting: no
Earliest Outdoor Planting: after last frost
Additional Plantings: 2-week intervals until early summer for continuous harvest
Last Planting: not needed

Preparing and Using

Cilantro leaves and coriander seeds are both used in curries and pickles. The strong, spicy leaves can be added to salads, fish, or beans, and it is found as an ingredient in many ethnic recipes. The stalks are also edible and have the same flavor as the leaves. Some cooks like to include the diced stalks to add some texture to the leaves, which wilt and go flat when exposed to heat or acidic liquids. The milder, sweeter coriander seeds can be ground and used in breads or cakes.

Problems

Cilantro is usually pest- and disease-free. The plant does suffer in humid, rainy weather.

All About Corn

Corn is a long-time favorite of most gardeners. The taste of store-bought corn can't compete with homegrown corn, so many gardeners plant a whole 4 × 4 SFG of just corn. Most of the varieties for home use are planted four per square foot; only one crop can be grown per season because it needs a long time to mature and lots of hot weather. There are many colors and varieties of corn. The later season types taste better than the earlier season varieties.

CORN

BOTANICAL INFORMATION
- **Family:** Grass
- **Height:** 5 to 6 feet
- **Spacing:** 4 per square

GROWING SEASON
- **Spring:** no
- **Summer:** yes
- **Fall:** no
- **Winter:** no

Seed to Harvest/Flower: 9 to 13 weeks
Seeds Storage: 1 to 2 years
Weeks to Maturity: 9 weeks
Indoor Seed Starting: no
Earliest Outdoor Planting: immediately after last spring frost
Additional Plantings: every 2 weeks

Starting

- Location: Full sun; locate corn where it won't shade other crops because it gets so tall.
- Seeds Indoors: No.
- Transplanting: Does not transplant well.
- Seeds Outdoors: Sprouts in five to ten days outdoors. Plant your presoaked seeds 1 to 2 inches deep, depending on the weather, at the proper spacing. To get a continuous harvest, plant a new crop every two weeks with several varieties of different maturation dates.

Growing

- Watering: Weekly, more in hot weather.
- Maintenance: Weed weekly; Place a raccoon-proof fence around your squares when the ears are starting to form.

Harvesting

- How: Use two hands to harvest—one to hold the stalk and the other to pull down and break off the ear—otherwise you may break the stalk. If there are no other ears left on that stalk it's best to cut it down to the ground. Don't pull it out or you may disturb the roots of the surrounding stalks.
- When: Check the ears daily when the silk first browns and the ears feel full and slightly bumpy. The final test of each ear before harvesting is to peel away a small strip of the husk to expose the kernels. They should be plump and full. To see if the ear is ready, puncture a kernel with your thumbnail. If milky juice squirts out, it's ready; if the juice is clear, the corn is not quite ready to pick.

Preparing and Using

Corn loses its sweet taste very quickly after being picked, so try to cook and eat it as soon as possible. If you can't use it immediately, husk and refrigerate it. Up to 50 percent of the flavor is lost in the first 12 hours of storage; more if it's not refrigerated. If you harvest more than you eat, cut the kernels off the cob and freeze them.

Problems

Corn has more problems than any other garden crop, including corn borer, ear worm, birds, raccoons, and squirrels.

All About Cucumbers

The cucumber is a garden favorite, and is very easy to grow in warm weather. Although both vine and bush varieties are available, bush cucumbers take a lot of room and don't produce like the vine types. Use the vertical method to grow your vine cucumbers. There are many varieties ranging in size, shape, and use, including ones for pickling or serving raw. The pickling varieties are picked much earlier when they are smaller—just the right size for the pickle jar—but they can also be eaten. The slicing types are grown larger.

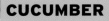

CUCUMBER

BOTANICAL INFORMATION
Family: Gourd
Height: vine
Spacing: 2 per square
GROWING SEASON
Spring: no
Summer: yes
Fall: no
Winter: no

Seed to Harvest/Flower: 9 weeks
Seeds Storage: 5 to 6 years
Weeks to Maturity: 7 weeks
Earliest Outdoor Planting: 1 week after last spring frost

Starting

- Location: Full sun, although the vine types will tolerate some shade.
- Seeds Indoors: Sprouts in four to eight days at 70°F; will sprout even faster at 80°F. Plant one seed in individual paper cups filled with Mel's Mix. Punch holes in the bottom for drainage. Keep warm (at least 70°F) until sprouted; move to full sunlight as soon as the first shoots appear.
- Transplanting: Plant the cup and all in the ground at the proper plant spacing. If the cup is waxed cardboard or a heavy paper, tear away the bottom carefully; avoid disturbing the roots.
- Seeds Outdoors: Sprouts in five to ten days; place presoaked seeds at proper spacing, water, and keep soil moist until seeds sprout.

Growing

- Watering: Weekly; twice weekly in hot weather. Never let the soil dry out. Avoid wetting the leaves, as this spreads any fungus disease that may be present. Cucumbers have the highest water content of any vegetable, so plenty of moisture is required for proper growth.

- Maintenance: Weed weekly; keep vines on the trellis; watch out for beetles; mulch in hot weather.

Harvesting

- How: Cut (don't pull) the stem connecting the fruit to the vine.
- When: Harvest continually! Never allow any cucumbers to become yellow or overly large, or the plant will stop producing. Keep picking even if you have to toss some on the compost pile because you can't use them. Don't try the old practice of eating the large cukes and leaving the smaller ones on the vine, because in only one or two days the little ones will be big. Instead, compost the very large cucumbers and eat the smaller ones.

Preparing and Using

Wash and scrub with a vegetable brush. Serve long, slender burpless varieties with the skins left on. Peel the fatter varieties before slicing, cubing, or cutting into long sticks. Serve fresh, sliced on sandwiches with onions and mayonnaise, or marinate for relish.

Problems

Cucumber beetles; mildew, wilt, and mosaic.

All About Eggplant

Eggplant is a nice-looking plant with fruit that comes in a wide variety of colors and shapes; most types yield a rather large, egg-shaped fruit that is black to purple. However, some of the newer varieties are yellow, brown, or white and are smaller and rounder. Eggplant yields a very large harvest and are used in many different styles of cooking. They are easily grown, but take a long time to mature—so you need to start plants indoors in early spring or buy transplants locally.

EGGPLANT

BOTANICAL INFORMATION
  Family: Nightshade
  Height: 24 to 30 inches
  Spacing: 1 per square
GROWING SEASON
  Spring: no
  Summer: yes
  Fall: no
  Winter: no

Seed to Harvest/Flower: 19 weeks
Seeds Storage: 5 to 6 years
Weeks to Maturity: 10 weeks
Indoor Seed Starting: 7 weeks before last spring frost
Earliest Outdoor Planting: 2 weeks after last spring frost
Additional Plantings: no

Starting

- Location: Full sun and lots of heat; pick your sunniest spot for eggplant.
- Seeds Indoors: Sprouts in twelve days at 70°F, but only requires six days at 85°F; won't sprout below 65°F. Sprinkle 5 to 10 seeds ¼ inch deep in a cup filled with vermiculite seven weeks before your last spring frost. Keep warm (at least 70°F) until sprouted; move to full sunlight as soon as first shoots appear; then pot up in seedling trays as soon as plants are large enough (usually one to three weeks).
- Transplanting: Plant into the garden two weeks after the last spring frost; disturb the roots as little as possible. Since eggplant is so vulnerable to cold weather, cover with a clear plastic cover to provide a greenhouse atmosphere if it is chilly.
- Seeds Outdoors: Not satisfactory, as the season is too short before hot weather arrives.

Growing

- Watering: Eggplant needs constant moisture, especially when fruits are forming and enlarging.
- Maintenance: Weed weekly; add a thick mulch when hot weather sets in. Provide a wide mesh, open-wire cage support when the eggplant is half grown; the plants will grow right through it, and will be supported without staking.

Harvesting

- How: Always cut the fruit from the bush with clippers.
- When: Edible almost anytime after the fruit turns dark and glossy (when it's about 6 inches); don't let them get too large. If they turn a dull color they are overripe and the seeds will be large and hard.

Preparing and Using

Peel and slice or dice, then stew, fry, stir-fry, or bake; add to casseroles, or bread and fry by itself. Eggplant mixes especially well with tomatoes and onions. If you're not going to use the eggplant right away, don't refrigerate it; instead, store it on the kitchen counter and enjoy its good looks! Handle carefully or fruit will bruise.

Problems

Cutworms and flea beetles; verticillium wilt.

All About Lettuce

Lettuce grows quickly and abundantly. It grows best in the cool seasons and withstands cold weather, but it can tolerate some heat. There are several types of lettuce:

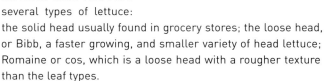

LETTUCE

BOTANICAL INFORMATION
   Family: Composite
   Height: 6 to 12 inches
   Spacing: 4 per square
GROWING SEASON
   Spring: yes
   Summer: yes
   Fall: yes
   Winter: yes

Seed to Harvest/Flower: 7 weeks
Seeds Storage: 5 to 6 years
Weeks to Maturity: 4 to 7 weeks
Indoor Seed Starting: 7 weeks before last spring frost
Earliest Outdoor Planting: 4 weeks before last spring frost
Additional Plantings: every other week
Last Planting: early summer

the solid head usually found in grocery stores; the loose head, or Bibb, a faster growing, and smaller variety of head lettuce; Romaine or cos, which is a loose head with a rougher texture than the leaf types.

Starting

- Location: Full sun to partial shade; shade is welcomed in the hot summer.
- Seeds Indoors: Sprouts in two to three days at 70°F. Start 5 to 10 seeds of several different varieties in cups filled with vermiculite seven weeks before your last spring frost date. Keep warm (70°F) until sprouted; move to full sunlight as soon as first shoots appear; then pot up in seedling trays as soon as plants are large enough (usually one to three weeks).
- Transplanting: Move plants into the garden anytime until they are half grown. Plant a new square or two of lettuce every other week until early summer.
- Seeds Outdoors: Sprouts in five to ten days. Seeds sprout quickly outdoors and grow fairly rapidly. Transplants seem to bolt to seed more easily than direct-seeded plants, so plant the summer crop directly in the garden. Plant one or two seeds in each hole; water daily until they sprout.

Growing

- Watering: Try not to wet the leaves; you may spread fungal diseases. Don't water at night; morning is the best followed by noon or late afternoon.

- Maintenance: Weed weekly; don't let any weeds grow. Lettuce has such a shallow root system it can't compete with weeds. Provide shade covers for plants in summer.

Harvesting

- How: You can cut individual outer leaves starting when the plant is half grown. If you take just one leaf from each plant, you can still harvest a lot and hardly notice what has been harvested.
- When: Harvest leaf varieties at seven weeks, and Bibb varieties at nine weeks, or harvest outer leaves from either one when the plant is half grown. You can also cut the entire plant at any time; it doesn't have to grow to full size to be edible.

Preparing and Using

Rinse lettuce under cool water, spin or pat dry, and store in the refrigerator in a plastic bag. Lettuce will stay fresh and crisp for several days. Lettuce contains vitamins A and B, calcium, and iron (especially the dark green outer leaves).

Problems

Rabbits, deer, woodchucks, slugs, cutworms, sow bugs, and wire worms. There are not many diseases to be concerned about.

All About Melons

Melons need about three months of hot weather to grow, but are a fun and exciting crop—even though the yield isn't large, when the harvest finally comes. They should be grown on vertical frames, as they will mature sooner and save space. Of course, one of the biggest rewards is seeing melons hanging 4 to 5 feet off the ground on your vertical frame.

MELON (CANTALOUPE, MUSKMELON, WATERMELON)

BOTANICAL INFORMATION
  Family: Gourd
  Height: vine
  Spacing: 1 per 2 squares
GROWING SEASON
  Spring: no
  Summer: yes
  Fall: no
  Winter: no

Seed to Harvest/Flower: 12 weeks
Seeds Storage: 5 to 6 years
Indoor Seed Starting: 2 weeks before transplanting
Earliest Outdoor Planting: 2 weeks after last spring frost
Additional Plantings: no

Starting

- Location: Full sun; grow on a vertical frame.
- Seeds Indoors: Sprouts in five to ten days at 70°F; the hotter the better, even up to 90°F for sprouting. Plant single seeds in individual paper cups. Plants do not transplant well, so don't start them until two weeks before planting outside.
- Transplanting: Plant outdoors two weeks after the last frost date. Sink the entire cup in the ground after tearing off the bottom.
- Seeds Outdoors: Won't sprout in soil below 65°F; takes five days in 70°F soil. Plant a pre-soaked seed in each square foot, one week after last frost. Cover with a plastic-covered cage. Remove weakest one later.

Growing

- Watering: Mulch heavily in hot weather. Reduce water when melons are almost ripe to develop their sweetness. Keep the leaves dry to avoid fungal diseases and mildew.
- Maintenance: Weed weekly; support the half-grown melons in slings; pinch out all new, small melons near the end of the growing season so that all the plant's strength goes into ripening the larger melons that are already set.

Harvesting

- How: Twist the melon with one hand while holding the stem with the other. If it resists parting, the melon is not ripe.

- When: Harvest whenever it has a strong melon scent, and the netting pattern on the rind (if it's a cantaloupe) becomes very prominent. The stem will slip off easily when the melon is rotated. If each melon is held in a sling it won't roll around and accidentally twist itself off when it's ripe.

Preparing and Using

Some people like melons warm, some like them chilled. Cut muskmelons or cantaloupes in half, scoop out the seeds, and cut into wedges, or serve an entire half filled with ice cream, blueberries, or custard. The flesh of all melons can also be scooped out using a melon-baller or cut into cubes and mixed with or added to a fresh fruit salad. They're excellent for breakfast or served as a dinner dessert.

Problems

Cutworms; mildew and wilt disease.

All About Onions

Onions are easy to grow; they don't take much care but are a little unsightly near the end when the tops turn brown and fall over—but that just means they are nearing harvest time. Onions can be planted from sets, plants, or seeds; the bulb reaches harvest sometime in the middle of the summer. The size of the bulb is determined by the length of the growing season before the summer solstice (June 21). If you have a short growing season, don't bother with seeds—get the plants or sets.

ONION

BOTANICAL INFORMATION
Family: Lily
Height: 12 inches
Spacing: 16 per square

GROWING SEASON
Spring: yes
Summer: yes
Fall: no
Winter: no

Seed to Harvest/Flower: 20 weeks
Seeds Storage: 1 to 2 years
Weeks to Maturity: 14 weeks
Indoor Seed Starting: 8 to 12 weeks before last spring frost
Earliest Outdoor Planting: 4 weeks before last spring frost

Starting

- Location: Onions like a sunny spot, but will tolerate some shade.
- Seeds Indoors: Sprouts in five days at 70°F. Sprinkle about 20 seeds into cups filled with vermiculite eight to twelve weeks before your last spring frost. Keep warm (70°F) until sprouted; move to full sunlight as soon as first shoots appear; then pot up in seedling trays as soon as plants are large enough (1 to 3 weeks).
- Transplanting: Four weeks before the last spring frost, shake the vermiculite from the plants and gather them in small bunches. With scissors, cut off the tops and roots so the plant has about 2 inches of each. Make a hole at each space in your square with a pencil, slip in a plant, and firm the soil.
- Seeds Outdoors: If the season is not long enough for seeds, use sets. Push the tiny onion sets into the ground, pointed side up at the proper spacing, with their tops just showing above the soil.

Growing

- Watering: Withhold water when the tops start to fall over.
- Maintenance: Weed weekly; when bulbs start expanding remove some of the soil around each bulb and partially uncover it. It will not hurt if you can actually see the top of every bulb; in fact, it's exciting to see them get bigger every week!

Harvesting

- How: Pull the onions and place on chicken wire or a window screen in the sun for several days. Brush them off then store for later use. Any onions with green or thick tops should not be stored but used immediately.
- When: About mid-summer the onion tops start to turn brown and fall over. When the majority have fallen, bend over the rest with your hand. In a short while, the tops will dry as the bulbs reach maximum size.

Preparing and Using

Homegrown onions are much milder and sweeter than store-bought ones. Hang dried onions in a mesh bag, or braid tops together and hang in a cool, dry area for storage all winter.

Problems

Onion fly maggot. Resistant to most diseases.

All About Oregano

What would Italian food be without a sprinkling of oregano to give it flavor and color? Oregano is a native of the Mediterranean area and enjoys lots of sunshine. It is a pretty plant with round leaves tightly covering the stems. Variegated oregano is particularly lovely with the leaves edged in white or gold, but the variegated plants are not quite as hardy as the all-green ones and are used mostly as ornamental plants. Give oregano frequent trimmings to keep it neat and so you can dry the leaves. It is one of few herbs whose flavor is stronger dried than fresh. When the leaves have dried, crumble them lightly and store in an airtight container.

OREGANO

BOTANICAL INFORMATION	
Family: Mint	**Seed to Harvest/Flower:** 16 weeks; hardy perennial
Height: 1 to 2 feet	**Seeds Storage:** n/a
Spacing: 1 per square	**Weeks to Maturity:** 8 to 10 weeks
GROWING SEASON	**Indoor Seed Starting:** 6 weeks before last spring frost
Spring: yes	**Earliest Outdoor Planting:** after last frost
Summer: yes	**Additional Plantings:** anytime throughout growing season
Fall: yes	**Last Planting:** not needed
Winter: no	

Starting

- Location: Full sun.
- Seeds Indoors: four to six weeks before last spring frost.
- Transplanting: Plant divisions anytime after the temperatures reach 45°F.
- Seeds Outdoors: Spring, after last frost; seeds need light to germinate.

Growing

- Watering: Weekly.
- Maintenance: Water sparingly; too much water will cause root rot. Harvest or trim mature plants often to keep them in bounds. Divide every two to three years.

Harvesting

- How: Cut stems back to a pair of leaves. This is where new branches will form.
- When: Oregano can be harvested anytime during the summer months, but the flavor is best after the buds have formed but just before the flowers open.

Preparing and Using

Oregano loses its distinctive flavor during cooking, so always add it in the last few minutes. Use oregano in salads, casseroles, soups, sauces, poultry dishes, and of course, pizza. Dried oregano has a stronger flavor than fresh and goes especially well with tomato or rice dishes.

Problems

Oregano is usually pest- and disease-free. Too much water can cause root rot.

All About Parsley

Parsley is a wonderful herb that looks great in the garden, yields a big continuous harvest, is extremely nutritious, and doesn't need a great deal of care! Pests don't seem to bother it, and it's disease-resistant too. All in all, parsley is a very easy addition to your SFG. There are many varieties, but basically two kinds: flat-leaved and curly. It's said the flat-leaf varieties taste better, but the curly-leaf types are better looking, and more commonly grown.

Starting

- Location: Full sun to partial shade.
- Seeds Indoors: Sprouts in ten to fifteen days at 70°F. Seeds are very slow to germinate, and should be soaked in lukewarm water for 24 hours before planting. Sprinkle ten presoaked seeds in a cup filled with vermiculite twelve weeks before last spring frost. Keep warm (70°F) until sprouted; move to full sunlight as soon as first shoots appear; then pot up in seedling trays as soon as plants are large enough (usually one to three weeks).
- Transplanting: Move outdoors five weeks before the last spring frost or anytime plants are large enough; plant them at the same depth they grew in the pot.
- Seeds Outdoors: Better to start indoors because seeds are slow and difficult to germinate.

Growing

- Watering: Never let parsley dry out completely because it becomes tough and bitter and may bolt to seed in the first year.
- Maintenance: Weed weekly. Mulch heavily for continual harvest in winter, and for early-spring growing the following year.

PARSLEY

BOTANICAL INFORMATION
- **Family:** Carrot
- **Height:** 6 to 12 inches
- **Spacing:** 4 per square

GROWING SEASON
- **Spring:** yes
- **Summer:** yes
- **Fall:** yes
- **Winter:** yes

Seed to Harvest/Flower: 14 weeks
Seeds Storage: 2 to 3 years
Weeks to Maturity: 7 weeks
Indoor Seed Starting: 12 weeks before last spring frost
Earliest Outdoor Planting: 5 weeks before last spring frost

Harvesting

- How: Cut outer leaves as needed; for a large harvest, cut off the entire plant slightly above tiny middle shoots. Either way, the plant will continue to grow with no harm.
- When: Harvest as soon as the plant gets 3 to 4 inches tall and anytime thereafter.

Preparing and Using

Parsley is good in soups, casseroles, stews, and with fish or any kind of meat; it's excellent over boiled vegetables, particularly potatoes. Parsley is loaded with vitamins A and C. Cut up leaves with scissors and sprinkle on food for that decorative gourmet chef look!

Problems

Relatively free from pests and diseases.

All About Peas

Who doesn't like the taste of fresh peas? Yet until the introduction of sugar snap peas, it was hard to grow enough for much more than a few meals. Sugar snaps have about five times the harvest of conventional peas and you can eat the entire pod. They are juicy, sweet, and crisp, and can be eaten raw or cooked. They are a must in my garden, and I recommend them as the only pea worth growing. Very few of the pea pods even make it to the kitchen now, because they are such a treat to eat right in the garden.

Starting

- Location: Full sun in spring; shaded toward summer if possible.
- Seeds Indoors: No.
- Transplanting: Does not transplant well.
- Seeds Outdoors: Sprouts in ten to fifteen days outdoors. Mix presoaked seeds with legume inoculant powder for an added boost, then plant 1 inch deep about five weeks before the last spring frost. Water and cover with a plastic-covered tunnel.

Growing

- Watering: Never let the peas dry out.
- Maintenance: Weed weekly; keep water off the vines. Keep the vines trained up the vertical frame; mulch as weather gets warm.

Harvesting

- How: Carefully (with two hands) pick or cut pods off their stems.
- When: The beauty of these peas is that you can eat them at any stage of growth. They're just as tasty (raw or cooked) whether their pods are fully mature and bulging with peas, or still thin and barely starting to show the peas inside. Munch on a few every time you're in the garden—what a treat!

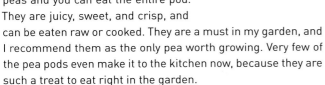

PEA, SUGAR SNAP

BOTANICAL INFORMATION
- **Family:** Pulse
- **Height:** vine
- **Spacing:** 8 per square

GROWING SEASON
- **Spring:** yes
- **Summer:** no
- **Fall:** yes
- **Winter:** no

- **Seed to Harvest/Flower:** 10 weeks
- **Seeds Storage:** 3 to 4 years
- **Weeks to Maturity:** 10 weeks
- **Indoor Seed Starting:** no
- **Earliest Outdoor Planting:** 5 weeks before last spring frost

Preparing and Using

Just wash and they are ready to eat or cook. Try to use them as fresh as possible; store what you can't use right away in refrigerator. Sugar snaps are rich in vitamins A, B1, and C, and contain phosphorus and iron. As the pods get nearly full size, some develop a string along each edge, but it's easy to remove: just snap off the stem end and pull down, and both strings will easily peel off. The pod is still very crisp and tasty even when full size.

If the pods start to lose their nice pea-green color and turn brown on the vine, they are overripe. Pick them immediately and add them to the compost pile, because if you don't harvest them they will cause the vine to stop producing new peas.

Problems

No pests to speak of, but sometimes prone to powdery mildew, especially during warm weather when the leaves get wet.

All About Peppers

Most gardeners love to grow peppers: they're easy to grow, pest- and disease-free, and produce a lot for the space allotted. You can buy transplants locally, or start seeds yourself. They look great in the garden, and some people grow several types for their decorative aspect. If all you've grown are the green bell peppers, give the sweet yellow banana varieties a try. Peppers come in several different shapes, from the bell shape to the skinny, curved, hot chili peppers. They range in color from green and red to orange and yellow.

PEPPER

BOTANICAL INFORMATION
- **Family:** Nightshade
- **Height:** 12 to 24 inches
- **Spacing:** 1 per square

GROWING SEASON
- **Spring:** no
- **Summer:** yes
- **Fall:** no
- **Winter:** no

Seed to Harvest/Flower: 19 weeks
Seeds Storage: 4 to 5 years
Weeks to Maturity: 10 weeks
Indoor Seed Starting: 7 weeks before last spring frost
Earliest Outdoor Planting: 2 weeks after last spring frost

Starting

- Location: Full sun.
- Seeds Indoors: Sprouts in ten to fifteen days at 70°F. Sprinkle 5 to 10 seeds in a cup of vermiculite approximately seven weeks before the last spring frost, cover with ¼ inch more vermiculite. Keep warm (70°F) until sprouted; move to full sunlight as soon as first shoots appear; then pot up in seedling trays as soon as plants are large enough (usually one to three weeks).
- Transplanting: Peppers need warm soil so don't transplant until two weeks after the last spring frost.
- Seeds Outdoors: The season is too short to start outdoors.

Growing

- Watering: Don't wet the leaves; this causes fungal and wilt infections.
- Maintenance: Weed weekly; mulch in hot weather; cover half-grown plants with an open-mesh wire cage to support plants without staking. Stems and branches are brittle and break easily, so be careful.

Harvesting

- How: Carefully cut the fruit from the bush (don't pull or you'll accidentally break other branches). Leave about 1 inch of stem on each pepper for a longer storage life.
- When: Harvest at almost any stage of development. Basically, if you want green peppers pick them as soon as they are big enough for your use. You can leave them on the vine and they will turn red or yellow after they become full grown. Peppers can still be eaten when red or yellow; in fact, many people prefer them, as their taste is sweeter and not as spicy when they lose their green color. Hot chili peppers should turn color before you use them.

Preparing and Using

Use peppers raw or cooked. Peppers are excellent as a salad or casserole garnish. Cut them into strips, cubes, or thin slices as you would a tomato. Their shape is very attractive as a garnish. Peppers stuffed with a meat, rice, or vegetable mixture and then baked makes a great summer supper. Peppers are high in vitamins A and C.

Problems

Cutworms and flea beetles. No diseases to speak of except an occasional wilt or fungus problem.

All About Potatoes

Growing your own potatoes is the best way to sample the large variety of potato shapes, sizes, and colors. Harvest them early for small, tasty nuggets; or dig them later for large tubers to store over the winter. And the potato plant itself is bushy and pretty, doing double duty as an ornamental and an edible. The white flowers are the indicator that the small, new potatoes are ready to harvest.

POTATO

BOTANICAL INFORMATION
Family: Nightshade
Height: 12 to 24 inches
Spacing: 4 per square
GROWING SEASON
Spring: yes
Summer: yes
Fall: yes
Winter: no

Seed to Harvest/Flower: 12 weeks
Seeds Storage: plant last year's potatoes each year
Weeks to Maturity: 12 weeks
Indoor Seed Starting: no
Earliest Outdoor Planting: in spring when soil has reached 45° F
Additional Plantings: late spring for a second crop to store over the winter

Starting

- Location: Full sun.
- Seeds Indoors: No.
- Planting: Don't plant seeds; cut up potatoes in small pieces and let the eyes sprout, then plant those.
- Outdoors: Plant in the spring when the soil has reached 45°F. Use only certified disease-free seed potatoes. Sprout potatoes a week before planting time by placing them in a tray where they will receive light (not sun) and temperatures of about 65°F. A day or two before planting, cut potatoes into "seed pieces" about 1½ inches square with at least one "sprouted eye" per section. Remove about 5 inches of your soil in that square foot, place four seed pieces at the proper spacing with eyes up, and just barely cover them. When sprouts appear, add enough Mel's Mix to again cover the green leafy sprouts. Keep doing this until the hole is filled back to the top. Cover the plants every week or so with more Mel's Mix, until the plants begin to flower. Make certain any new potatoes that are forming are well covered, as uncovered spuds will turn green.

Growing

- Watering: Increase watering during flowering.

Maintenance: Protect from frost. Harvesting

- How: Gently loosen the soil around early potatoes and remove the largest tubers, leaving the smaller ones to continue growing. For later potatoes, gently dig outside the plant and remove the potatoes as you find them. Take care not to stab or cut the potatoes as you dig. Store potatoes in a cool (40°F), dark location for three to six months. Do not store potatoes near apples, which give off a chemical that will damage the potatoes.
- When: Small early potatoes can be harvested as needed in early summer after the plants finish flowering. Later potatoes can be left in the soil until two to three weeks after the foliage has died back in fall, and can be lifted all at once for storing.

Preparing and Using

Potatoes can be boiled, fried, steamed, grilled, or baked. All potatoes should be cooked or placed in water immediately after peeling to prevent discoloration.

Problems

Flea beetles, leaf hoppers, and slugs; blight, scab, and root knot nematode. Tubers exposed to sunlight turn green and are mildly toxic.

All About Radishes

Radishes are a great crop for all gardeners—from experts to beginners. Who can pass up a vegetable that matures in only three weeks? Plus, they are zesty and tasty in any dish. Radishes come in a multitude of shapes, from small and round to long carrot shapes. They vary in color from red, pink, white, and even some black varieties. Radishes planted in the spring are normally red or white colored, and will mature in three to four weeks. Fall radishes take six to eight weeks and store very well; they're referred to as winter radishes.

Starting

- Location: Full sun to partial shade.
- Seeds Indoors: No.
- Transplanting: Does not transplant well.
- Seeds Outdoors: Sprouts in five to ten days outdoors depending on temperature. Plant a square foot every other week for a staggered but continuous harvest. Plant ½ inch deep in spring, 1 inch deep in summer. If you really like radishes a lot, plant some every week of the growing year, even through the hot weather. The plants will still do fairly well then if you give them some shade, lots of water, and a thick mulch. Winter or long-keeping varieties need two months to mature, so start them at least that long before the first fall frost.

Growing

- Watering: Don't let radishes stop growing or dry out; lack of water causes hot-tasting and pithy radishes.
- Maintenance: Weed weekly; keep covered with screen-covered cage if root maggots are a problem; mulch in hot weather.

RADISH

BOTANICAL INFORMATION	
Family: Mustard	**Seed to Harvest/Flower:** 4 weeks
Height: 6 to 12 inches	**Seeds Storage:** 5 to 6 years
Spacing: 16 per square	**Weeks to Maturity:** 3 weeks
GROWING SEASON	**Indoor Seed Starting:** no
Spring: yes	**Earliest Outdoor Planting:** 3 weeks before last spring frost
Summer: yes	**Additional Plantings:** every other week
Fall: yes	
Winter: no	

Harvesting

- How: Pull up the entire plant and trim off the top. Refrigerate edible portions if they're not used immediately.
- When: Harvest as soon as they are marble size up to Ping-Pong ball size; the smaller you pull them, the sweeter they taste. The long fall varieties can be left in the ground until frost, then either mulched to keep the ground from freezing, or pulled and stored in damp peat moss or sand after the tops are removed.

Preparing and Using

Slice, dice, or cut into fancy shapes for eating out of hand or to add to salads, and for garnishes. If you have too many all at once, twist or cut off the tops and store in a plastic bag in the refrigerator. Radishes will keep for up to a week before getting soft.

Problems

None to speak of, except possibly root maggots.

All About Spinach

Spinach is somewhat difficult to grow, but it is a very popular plant. It usually does well if it stays cool in the spring. A rapid grower, it can be grown in a fairly small space and looks great in the garden. It will quickly bolt to seed in the summer heat, but grows very well in the early spring and then again in the fall. Spinach is very cold hardy and in many areas of the country it will winter over; in warmer climates, it can be grown all winter.

There are two types of spinach—the smooth-leaved kind and a crinkly-leaved type called Savoy, which is more popular and more attractive. Neither will endure heat and should be grown in cool weather. Some varieties are more resistant to frost and are particularly adaptable for growing in the fall, and possibly into the winter season. Check your seed catalog for appropriate varieties.

SPINACH

BOTANICAL INFORMATION	
Family: Goosefoot	**Seed to Harvest/Flower:** 7 weeks
Height: 6 to 12 inches	**Seeds Storage:** 5 to 6 years
Spacing: 9 per square	**Weeks to Maturity:** 7 weeks
GROWING SEASON	**Indoor Seed Starting:** no
Spring: yes	**Earliest Outdoor Planting:** 5 weeks before last spring frost
Summer: no	
Fall: yes	
Winter: yes	

Starting

- Location: Any location is suitable, full sun to partial shade.
- Seeds Indoors: No.
- Transplanting: Does not transplant well.
- Seeds Outdoors: Sprouts outdoors in one to two weeks. Plant seeds ½ inch deep, water, and cover with a plastic-covered cage. Plants can withstand any temperature between 25°F and 75°F, so judge your spring and fall planting accordingly.

Growing

- Watering: Being a leaf crop, spinach needs constant moist soil.
- Maintenance: Weed weekly; mulch in warm weather. Don't work in the spinach square if the leaves are very wet—they are brittle and break easily.

Harvesting

- How: Cut outer leaves as needed; small inner leaves will continue to grow rapidly.
- When: Harvest as soon as the plants look like they won't miss an outer leaf or two. Keep picking and the plant will keep growing right up until hot weather. If it's a spring crop and you think the plants are going to bolt soon, cut off the entire plant for a little extra harvest.

Preparing and Using

Wash carefully; soil tends to cling to the undersides, especially on the ones with crinkled leaves. Spin or pat dry and store in refrigerator just like lettuce. Better yet, eat spinach right away. Serve fresh in salads, cook slightly for a wilted spinach salad, or cook by steaming lightly. Spinach goes great with any meal, especially when garnished with a chopped, hard-boiled egg. It's high in vitamins A, B1, and C, and is a valuable source of iron.

Problems

Leaf miners and aphids. No diseases to speak of.

All About Strawberries

Picking strawberries on a clear June day is a treat for young, old, and everyone in between—only about half the harvest actually makes it into the basket! Since strawberries are so popular, most families like to plant an entire SFG in strawberries—it's easy to protect and harvest. Strawberry plants bear fruit for at least three or four years, then yields will decrease and eventually the plant will die. There are three main types of strawberries: June-bearing, which sets fruit in June; ever-bearing, which will set fruit twice during the growing season; and day-neutral, which is not affected by the length of the day as the others are. And don't overlook the Alpine strawberry, which will reward you with tiny but incredibly tasty fruit over a long period!

STRAWBERRY

BOTANICAL INFORMATION
Family: Rose
Height: 6 to 12 inches
Spacing: 4 per square
GROWING SEASON
Spring: yes
Summer: no
Fall: yes
Winter: no

Seed to Harvest/Flower: n/a
Seeds Storage: no; seed-started plants take up to 3 years to bear fruit
Weeks to Maturity: n/a
Earliest Outdoor Planting: 4 weeks before last spring frost

Starting

- Location: Full sun.
- Seeds Indoors: No.
- Transplanting: Early spring, as soon as the soil is not frozen. Be sure soil is not wet.
- Outdoors: Most gardeners buy strawberry plants in packets of a dozen or so. Soak first, then trim off the roots slightly, and plant four per square foot. Leave a saucer-shaped depression around each plant for effective watering. Keep the soil moist; increase water when strawberries are fruiting.

Growing

- Watering: Weekly; more during dry periods.
- Maintenance: Cut off all the runners as soon as you see them each week; that way all the energy will stay in the parent plant for an increased harvest each year. After three or four years when the harvest starts to diminish, it is best to pull out those plants and replant, perhaps in a different square with brand-new certified disease-free plants

from the nursery. It's true that those runners will produce baby plants and it seems a waste not to use them. However, the problem comes from too many runners producing too many baby plants that take all the energy from the parent, reducing the harvest.

Harvesting

How: Pick the fruit leaving a short piece of stem attached; use scissors for a clean cut.
When: Harvest as fruit ripens, for two to three weeks.

Preparing and Using

Use strawberries as soon as possible after picking; pop a few right in your mouth. They can be used in fruit salads, on cakes, and in pies. Freeze whole strawberries for use in smoothies—they will be soft when they defrost, but still flavorful.

Problems

Birds and slugs; verticillium wilt. People who put too many in their mouth and too few in the basket.

All About Summer Squash

Summer squash needs a lot of room to grow, but is unbelievably prolific. It is easy and fast to grow, but needs hot weather to do well. There are many colors and shapes—round, straight, crookneck, and flat—each with its particular taste.

Most of the varieties sold are the bush types (especially zucchini), so you'll have to assign a larger space (a 3 × 3 area) to just one plant. However, those plants can produce a vast amount of fruit, so most gardeners think it's worthwhile, at least for one or two plants.

An alternate solution is to grow the vining types on vertical frames, which is quite a space saver. Zucchini can be trained to grow vertically, but it still takes a lot of room because of those huge leaves and prickly stems. Check the seed packet or catalog to make sure you are getting a vine type.

Starting

- Location: Full sun.
- Seeds Indoors: Doesn't transplant well because of the long taproot. It's best to start seeds outdoors. If you do want to start indoors, plant one seed in a paper cup of Mel's Mix 1 inch deep. Plant two weeks before your last frost date.
- Transplanting: Plant outdoors on your last spring frost date.
- Seeds Outdoors: Sprouts in five to ten days outdoors. For bush types, plant two presoaked seeds in the center of a nine-square space. For vine types, also plant two presoaked seeds in the middle of a 2-square-foot space under your vertical frame. Make sure you hollow out a dish shape around the planted seeds to hold plenty of water. Place a plastic-covered cage over the seeds to warm the soil. After sprouting, cut off the weakest plant if both seeds sprout.

SUMMER SQUASH

BOTANICAL INFORMATION
- **Family:** Gourd
- **Height:** bush or vine
- **Spacing:**
  Bush: 1 per 9 square feet
  Vine: 1 per 2 square feet

GROWING SEASON
- **Spring:** no
- **Summer:** yes
- **Fall:** no
- **Winter:** no

Seed to Harvest/Flower: 8 weeks
Seeds Storage: 5 to 6 years
Weeks to Maturity: 6 to 8 weeks
Indoor Seed Starting: 2 weeks before last spring frost
Earliest Outdoor Planting: immediately following last spring frost

Growing

- Watering: Keep the leaves dry to prevent powdery mildew.
- Maintenance: Weed weekly; keep vines trained up vertical frames or within bounds of the square.

Harvesting

- How: Carefully cut through the fruit stem but do not cut the main vine or leaf stems. Handle the squash gently as their skins are very soft and easily damaged by fingernails or if dropped.
- When: Harvest as soon as the blossoms wilt, and until the fruits are 6 to 9 inches long. Don't let them grow any longer. Sometimes you have to harvest at least three times a week; they grow that fast. Squash loses flavor as the seeds inside mature.

Preparing and Using

Rinse lightly and serve sliced or cut into sticks, with a dip, or just as an appetizer anytime. Cook lightly by steaming or stir-frying, in any number of dishes or combinations. Serve squash by itself or with other vegetables, seasoned with a little dressing, grated cheese, or chopped parsley. Squash is high in vitamins A, B1, and C.

Problems

Squash vine borer and squash bug; powdery mildew.

All About Winter Squash

A space-hogging plant that many gardeners won't grow because of its large leaves and rampaging vines, winter squash can take over the entire garden. That's why we grow it vertically. The fruit can be picked in the late fall and stored without difficulty to be used during the winter; it retains its delectable flavor long after being harvested. There are many varieties to select from, but butternut and acorn are the most popular. All winter squashes have thick skins that harden in the fall, and are generally picked after the vines have been killed by frost. You don't get your compensation until season's end, but since there is almost no fresh produce then, the winter squash is very welcomed. The fruit has a mild flavor and is fine grained.

Starting

- Location: Full sun, but tolerates a little shade.
- Seeds Indoors: No.
- Transplanting: Does not transplant well because of the long taproot.
- Seeds Outdoors: Since the seeds sprout quickly, you might as well start them outdoors. Plant two presoaked seeds in the center of 2 square feet. Make sure you've left a 2-inch depression around the seeds to hold lots of water during the season. Cover with a plastic covered cage to warm the soil and encourage fast seed sprouting. Cut off the weakest plant if both seeds sprout.

Growing

- Watering: Keep soil moist.
- Maintenance: Weed weekly; keep vines trained up the vertical frame.

WINTER SQUASH

BOTANICAL INFORMATION
Family: Gourd
Height: vine
Spacing: 1 per 2 square feet
GROWING SEASON
Spring: no
Summer: yes
Fall: no
Winter: no

Seed to Harvest/Flower: 12 weeks
Seeds Storage: 5 to 6 years
Weeks to Maturity: 12 weeks
Indoor Seed Starting: no
Earliest Outdoor Planting: 2 weeks after last spring frost

Harvesting

- How: Cut the squash from the vine, leaving as long a stem as possible, at least 2 inches. Then set the fruit out in the sun to cure for a few days, protecting it at night when frost is in the forecast.
- When: Harvest after the first light frost, which will kill the leaves and vines, and after the main vine wilts, but before a very hard frost.

Preparing and Using

Peel, cut in half, scoop out seeds, and prepare for boiling or baking. Excellent served mashed or in chunks with butter and parsley. Winter squash can even be added to some soups and stews. Butternut can be used in pumpkin pie recipes (many cooks say it's better tasting than pumpkin itself). Store winter squash in a cool, dry place at 40° to 50°F; check often and use if you see any bruised or rotten spots.

Problems

A few beetles; powdery mildew; and vines too rambunctious to control.

All About Tomatoes

If you don't plant anything else, you should plant tomatoes. There is a huge selection available, some specifically suited for eating, juicing, cooking, or canning. They're available in early, midseason, or late types in different colors ranging from red, orange, pink, and yellow. Size also varies from the small cherry tomato to the extra large 4-pound types that win awards at the county fair.

TOMATO

BOTANICAL INFORMATION
Family: Nightshade
Height: bush, 3 feet tall; vine, 6 feet tall
Spacing:
Bush: 1 per 9 square feet
Vine: 1 per square foot

GROWING SEASON
Spring: no
Summer: yes
Fall: no
Winter: no

Seed to Harvest/Flower: 17 weeks
Seeds Storage: 4 to 5 years
Weeks to Maturity: 11 weeks
Indoor Seed Starting: 6 weeks before last spring frost
Outdoor Seed Starting: no
Earliest Outdoor Planting: immediately after last spring frost

Starting

- Location: Full sun.
- Seeds Indoors: Sprouts in one week at 70°F. Sprinkle five or so seeds of each variety you want to grow in individual cups filled with vermiculite six weeks before your last spring frost. Just barely cover with vermiculite and water; move to full sunlight as soon as first shoots appear. Then pot up in seedling trays or individual pots as soon as plants are large enough (usually one to three weeks).
- Transplanting: Harden off transplants for one to two weeks, and plant outside on or after your frost-free date. Plant one vine-type plant per square foot. Bush types are planted in the center of a nine-square-foot area. They take up so much room that I now grow only vine-type varieties.
- Seeds Outdoors: The season is too short to start outdoors.

Growing

- Watering: Keep water off the plant leaves.
- Maintenance: Prune off side branches (suckers) weekly for vine types and guide plant tops up through netting. Prune off lower dead or yellow leaves. Keep adding mulch as the season gets hotter.

Harvesting

- How: Gently twist and pull ripe tomatoes so the stem breaks (if it's ripe it should easily break away), or cut the stem so as not to disturb the rest of the remaining fruit.
- When: If you're not going to wait until they're red and ripe, why grow them yourself? Some gardeners like to pick them just slightly before that point (say a day or two) if they want extra-firm tomatoes for sandwiches or a particular dish. If you leave them on the vine too long they will turn soft and mushy, so inspect daily; it's one of the pleasures you've been waiting for all year.

Preparing and Using

Tomatoes can be used in a multitude of ways. You can enjoy sliced tomatoes seasoned with lots of pepper, or try pouring salad dressing over sliced tomatoes. Soak a plate full in vinegar overnight for the next day's treat. Add thick slices of fresh tomatoes to any casserole and enjoy a flavor not experienced the rest of the year.

Problems

Cutworm, whitefly, and the big, bad, but beautiful tomato horn worm; various wilt diseases.

Conversions

Metric Equivalent

Inches (in.)	1/64	1/32	1/25	1/16	1/8	1/4	3/8	2/5	1/2	5/8	3/4	7/8	1	2	3	4	5	6	7	8	9	10	11	12	36	39.4
Feet (ft.)																								1	3	3 1/12
Yards (yd.)																									1	1 1/12
Millimeters (mm)	0.40	0.79	1		1.59	3.18	6.35	9.53	10	12.7	15.9	19.1	22.2	25.4	50.8	76.2	101.6	127	152	178	203	229	254	279	305	914 · 1,000
Centimeters (cm)					0.95	1	1.27	1.59	1.91	2.22	2.54	5.08	7.62	10.16	12.7	15.2	17.8	20.3	22.9	25.4	27.9	30.5	91.4	100		
Meters (m)																						.30	.91	1.00		

Converting Measurements

TO CONVERT:	TO:	MULTIPLY BY:
Inches	Millimeters	25.4
Inches	Centimeters	2.54
Feet	Meters	0.305
Yards	Meters	0.914
Miles	Kilometers	1.609
Square inches	Square centimeters	6.45
Square feet	Square meters	0.093
Square yards	Square meters	0.836
Cubic inches	Cubic centimeters	16.4
Cubic feet	Cubic meters	0.0283
Cubic yards	Cubic meters	0.765
Pints (U.S.)	Liters	0.473 (Imp. 0.568)
Quarts (U.S.)	Liters	0.946 (Imp. 1.136)
Gallons (U.S.)	Liters	3.785 (Imp. 4.546)
Ounces	Grams	28.4
Pounds	Kilograms	0.454
Tons	Metric tons	0.907

TO CONVERT:	TO:	MULTIPLY BY:
Millimeters	Inches	0.039
Centimeters	Inches	0.394
Meters	Feet	3.28
Meters	Yards	1.09
Kilometers	Miles	0.621
Square centimeters	Square inches	0.155
Square meters	Square feet	10.8
Square meters	Square yards	1.2
Cubic centimeters	Cubic inches	0.061
Cubic meters	Cubic feet	35.3
Cubic meters	Cubic yards	1.31
Liters	Pints (U.S.)	2.114 (Imp. 1.76)
Liters	Quarts (U.S.)	1.057 (Imp. 0.88)
Liters	Gallons (U.S.)	0.264 (Imp. 0.22)
Grams	Ounces	0.035
Kilograms	Pounds	2.2
Metric tons	Tons	1.1

Converting Temperatures

Convert degrees Fahrenheit (F) to degrees Celsius (C) by following this simple formula: Subtract 32 from the Fahrenheit temperature reading. Then mulitply that number by 5/9. For example, 77°F - 32 = 45. 45 × 5/9 = 25°C.

To convert degrees Celsius to degrees Fahrenheit, multiply the Celsius temperature reading by 9/5, then add 32. For example, 25°C × 9/5 = 45. 45 + 32 = 77°F.

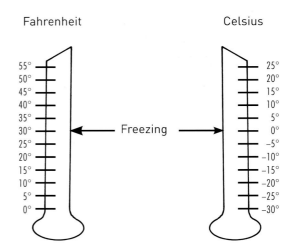

Fahrenheit · Celsius · Freezing

Resources

American Community Gardening Association (ACGA)
This non-profit organization promotes community gardening throughout the United States with educational and informational programs and materials. Gardeners will find advice, articles, and other information about starting community gardens, and other community gardening issues, on the website.
communitygarden.org
(877) 275-2242
info@communitygarden.org

Cooperative Extension System
This countrywide network of county offices is staffed by agricultural professionals that provide advice and answers regarding local growing conditions, pests, the best varieties to plant, and more.
www.csrees.usda.gov/Extension/
(202) 720-4423

J.W. Jung Seed Company
Jung is another long-time supplier of seeds, covering a wide range of categories that include a diversity of vegetable and fruit varieties. The website includes advice and information about choosing the right plants for your zone and yard.
www.jungseed.com
(800) 297-3123

Mel's Blog
You can find answers to other Square Foot Gardeners' questions on this blog, along with some wisdom and advice from the founder of Square Foot Gardening. There's more information here than you can shake a stick at, and kids can even ask a question themselves.
www.melbartholomew.com

Park Seed
Founded in 1868, Park Seed is one of the oldest mail-order seed and plant suppliers. They offer a full range of fruits, vegetables, flowers, and more.
Parkseed.com
(800) 845-3369

The Square Foot Gardening Foundation
A multi-faceted non-profit, the Foundation provides a forum for Square Foot Gardeners to learn more about SFG, exchange opinions and advice, ask questions, and purchase materials such as boxes and grids.
www.squarefootgardening.org

World Food Programme
A non-profit dedicated to solving world hunger, the WFP operates around the globe, with programs for teachers, students, parents, and other individuals. They offer many ways for any person to help fight world hunger, but have not yet embraced SFG as an overall solution. The website includes an interactive map of world hunger (cdn.wfp.org/hungermap).
www.wfp.org

Credits

Victoria Boudman: pp. 8, 49, 75, 79, 101, 103 (top left), 141, 147, 149, 151

LDI: pp. 95 (right), 156, 160, 161, 163, 164, 171, 177, 179, 181, 182

iStock: pp. 159

Paul Markert: pp. 4, 11, 14, 15, 17, 18, 32, 37, 41, 48, 50 (all), 51, 52, 56, 58 (both), 59 (top), 61 (both), 62, 69, 72, 77, 80, 81, 82 (all), 83, 87, 88, 91, 93 (right, top and lower), 96, 97 (right), 98, 99 (both), 104 (both), 105 (both), 112, 118 (all), 119 (all), 120, 128, 129 (both), 130 (both), 131 (both), 136, 154

J. Paul Moore: pp. 59 (lower), 63, 71, 93, 94 (both), 95 (left)

Shantlee Hope Sutch: pp. 6, 13 (both), 22, 23, 24, 25, 40, 42 (top), 54, 97 (left), 135, 138, 139, 153

Shutterstock: pp. 46, 57, 84, 86 (both), 89, 90, 107 (both), 114, 132, 133, 134, 152, 158, 162, 165, 166, 167, 168, 169, 170, 172, 173, 174, 175, 176, 178, 180, 183

Index

Meet Mel Bartholomew

Mel Bartholomew's path to arguably the most influential backyard gardener was an untraditional one. A civil engineer by profession and frustrated gardener by weekend, Bartholomew was convinced unmanageable single-row gardening was a waste of energy and output. After his research yielded responses such as "but that's the way we've always done it," Bartholomew condensed the unmanageable single-row space to 4 × 4 feet, amended the soil, and bingo . . . he developed a gardening system that yields 100 percent of the harvest in 20 percent of the space.

Bartholomew's Square Foot Method quickly gained popularity and strength, ultimately converting more than one million gardeners worldwide. Square Foot Gardening, the highest-rated PBS gardening show to date, launched in 1981 and ran weekly for five years, followed later by a weekly Square Foot Show on the Discovery Network. In 1986 the creation of the Square Foot Gardening Foundation and the "A Square Yard in the School Yard Program" brought the technique to an estimated three thousand schools nationwide.

As fan mail and testimonials from thousands of gardeners across the country arrived, Bartholomew realized that his Square Foot Method was relevant on a global scale. Converted into Square Meter Gardening, Bartholomew seized an opportunity to bring the dietary benefits of his revolutionary system to millions of malnourished Third World citizens. His global humanitarian effort, orchestrated through the Square Meter International Training Centers in Lehigh, Utah, and Homestead, Florida, trained international humanitarian organizations and leaders in the Square Meter Method. Since its launch, Bartholomew's global outreach initiative has spread from Africa to Asia to South America and is recognized as a resounding success by nonprofit human interest groups.

And there are no signs of slowing down. Bartholomew's global outreach continues throughout the world while closer to home, attention has shifted to increasing the Square Foot presence in the California school system. Bartholomew is determined to continue and strengthen the well established Square Foot programs and institutions across the nation and the globe.

Bartholomew operates his nonprofit Square Foot Gardening Foundation in Eden, Utah.